Cost Accounting and Management
Essentials You Always Wanted To Know

Self-Learning Management Series

 Vibrant Publishers

www.vibrantpublishers.com

Cost Accounting and Management
Essentials You Always Wanted To Know

ISBN-10: 1461127572
ISBN-13: 978-14-61127-57-4

Library of Congress Control Number: 2011928208

This publication is designed to provide accurate and authoritative information in regard to the subject matter covered. The author has made every effort in the preparation of this book to ensure the accuracy of the information. However, information in this book is sold without warranty either expressed or implied. The Author or the Publisher will not be liable for any damages caused or alleged to be caused either directly or indirectly by this book.

Vibrant Publishers books are available at special quantity discount for sales promotions, or for use in corporate training programs. For more information please write to **bulkorders@vibrantpublishers.com**

Please email feedback / corrections (technical, grammatical or spelling) to **spellerrors@vibrantpublishers.com**

To access the complete catalogue of Vibrant Publishers, visit **www.vibrantpublishers.com**

About the Author

Kalpesh Ashar, a management consultant and corporate trainer holds an M.B.A. (Dean's Award Winner) from S.P. Jain Institute of Management & Research, one of Asia's top B-Schools, and an Engineering degree with Honours in Electronics. He has over 13 years of experience in large corporations and start-ups in Asia, U.S.A and Europe.

Kalpesh has worked in the capacity of Senior Manager and Program Manager and is passionate about writing on management subjects. While mentoring managers and management students, he realized the need for a series of management books based on quick self-learning. He has authored this series that gives a jump start to managers in understanding all aspects of a business. His technology background gives him a good understanding of the management learning needs of non-M.B.A. graduates. Accordingly, he has authored the titles in this series in a simple to understand manner.

Kalpesh conducts corporate trainings in management subjects and also works as a management consultant for growing companies. He is also affiliated with top business schools in India as a visiting faculty. He is well known as a great mentor in the companies he has worked in and has also received "Best Manager" award.

For any queries regarding this book, Kalpesh can be directly reached at *kalpesh.ashar@vibrantpublishers.com*

Self-Learning Management Series

Financial Accounting Essentials
Cost Accounting & Management Essentials
Financial Management Essentials
Marketing Management Essentials
Consumer Buyer Behavior Essentials
Enterpreneurship Essentials
Organisational Behavior Essentials
Business Strategies Essentials
Principles of Management Essentials
Supply Chain Management Essentials

For updated list visit www.vibrantpublishers.com

Table of Contents

Cost Accounting and Management

Essentials You Always Wanted To Know

This page is intentionally left blank

CHAPTER 1:

Introduction

An accounting system helps capture and organize information related to business transactions. Depending upon the focus it can be divided into two types – Financial Accounting & Managerial Accounting. A Financial Accounting system contains financial statements and disclosures meant for decision makers external to the company. A Managerial Accounting system contains detailed plans and performance reports meant for decision makers within the company.

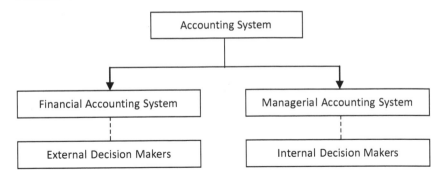

Cost Accounting provides information required by both types of accounting systems. Another term, Cost Management, is also used frequently. It refers to the approaches and activities adopted by managers to use the company's resources to increase the value given to customers and to achieve organizational goals. It must be noted that cost management is not synonymous with cost reduction.

In the later chapters we shall look at cost accounting and cost management aspects of accounting. We shall see how cost accounting information helps in short-term tactical and long-term strategic decision making.

Cost Accounting Terms

This section sets a foundation by describing the most important terms used in cost accounting. An understanding of these terms will help in later sections to understand how costs work, how they are reported and how decisions are taken using them.

Cost Object

Cost object is the product or service with respect to which cost needs to be computed. For example, if a car manufacturer wants to assess costs, the cars that they manufacture would be their cost object. Similarly, cost object for a bank would be customer accounts. Costs are classified below on the basis of the cost object. This classification is with respect to the cost object.

Direct and Indirect Costs

Costs are classified under two categories as below:

Direct Costs

These are costs that can be directly traced or caused by a product, service, project, organizational unit, or activity. For example, the cost of steering wheel is a direct cost in the manufacture of a car. Similarly, cost of effort put by a worker in making the doors of the car also amounts to direct cost. Below are some examples of direct cost.

a) Cost of cement used in construction of a building
b) Cost of tires used in building a car
c) Cost of project management consultant in bridge construction

Indirect Costs

These are costs that cannot be directly traced to a single product, service, project, organizational unit, or activity. These costs are allocated rather than being traced to individual products or services as there is no cost effective way of tracing them directly. This allocation can be done in several ways described in detail later. For example, rent of a plant used to manufacture cars of multiple varieties cannot be directly traced to every car model. Hence, the rent is an indirect cost. If the plant were to manufacture only one car model then the rent would become a direct cost. Similarly, cost of supervisors for various products of the company is also an indirect cost and needs to be allocated in some proportion instead of being directly traced to the products. Below are some examples of indirect costs.

a) Salary of staff in corporate headquarters
b) Cost of adhesive used in creating various products of the company. This is especially because it may not be cost effective to try and relate this cost directly to each product. It would be much better to allocate this cost on a certain basis (an estimation)
c) Cost of power in a plant making many different products

Variable and Fixed Costs

When a company changes the amount of products and/or services it provides, its total costs would also change. However, some costs change in relation to quantity or volume, whereas, others do not. On this basis, there are the following categories of costs.

Variable Costs

Costs that change proportionately with volume are called variable costs. So if the company sells 10% more products then its variable costs would also go up by 10%. For example, cost of car tires is variable and so is the cost of steering wheel. We saw earlier that both of these costs are also Direct costs. Hence, a certain cost can be Direct and at the same time, Variable. Below are some other examples of variable cost.

a) Cost of paint required for a house
b) Cost of labor for manufacturing a truck
c) Cost of wood in constructing a house

Below diagram and table show how variable costs behave

Units produced	Variable cost per unit	Total variable cost
10	$ 500	$ 5,000
50	$ 500	$ 25,000
200	$ 500	$ 100,000

Non-variable / Fixed Costs

These are exactly opposite of variable costs. They do not vary with the quantity or volume of product manufactured or service provided. This means that this cost is independent of the volume. For example, rent of office premises is a fixed cost as it does not change with the change in business volume. Below are some examples of fixed costs.

a) Cost of assembly line for a car model
b) Cost of supervisor
c) Cost of rent paid by a bank branch office

However, it may be noted that fixed costs are generally fixed within a certain relevant range. For example, if the business grows so much that a new office will have to be bought to accommodate the new machinery and personnel, then the rent cost changes. Hence, it is said to be fixed only over a certain volume of business called the relevant range. Below diagram and table show how fixed costs behave over the relevant range.

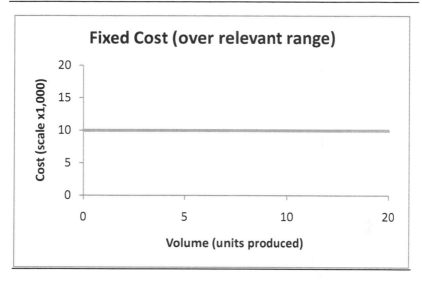

Total Fixed cost	Units produced	Fixed cost per unit
$ 10,000	5	$ 2,000
$ 10,000	10	$ 1,000
$ 10,000	20	$ 500

Fixed costs are generally chunky costs or a step-function, as they are incurred in chunks when one goes outside the relevant range. So if a new office is to be bought for additional space, the fixed cost would increase by a large chunk equal to the rent of the new office. It will then stay fixed until the business grows beyond another higher relevant range. Below diagram and table show how fixed costs behave across different relevant ranges.

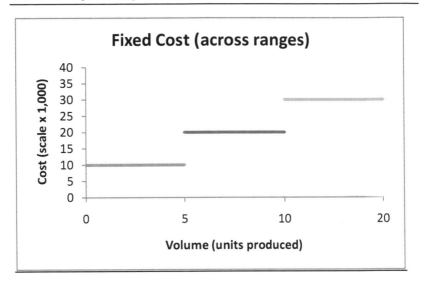

Total Fixed cost	Units produced	Fixed cost per unit
$ 10,000	3	$ 3,333
$ 10,000	4	$ 2,500
$ 20,000	6	$ 3,333
$ 20,000	7	$ 2,857
$ 30,000	11	$ 2,727
$ 30,000	15	$ 2,000

Semi-variable Costs

Several costs are a combination of both of the above. The total amount in such costs will then change with volume but not proportionately. It is always best to try and separate this into two components – fixed cost and variable cost, and deal with them separately. For example, telephone bills usually contain a fixed charge for having a connection and a variable charge based on actual usage. In this case it is easy to separate the two costs. Similarly, cost of driving a car contains many components, like cost of gasoline, oil, tires, and maintenance, all of which are variable. But there are also costs of insurance and registration that are fixed. Hence, the total cost in both the above cases is semi-variable and can be easily separated into its fixed and variable components.

The two distinctions of costs – Direct & Indirect and Variable & Fixed are on separate dimensions. Hence, every cost would be a combination of these. The following combinations are possible:

a) Direct and Variable – Cost of tires of car
b) Direct and Fixed – Rent of factory producing only one kind of car
c) Indirect and Variable – Cost of power in a factory producing several types of cars
d) Indirect and Fixed – Rent of factory producing several types of cars

Unit Costs

Several times costs are quoted on a per unit basis, like $5 per piece. This means that one piece costs $5. In this case $5 is a unit cost. However, there are important considerations while computing unit costs.

Firstly, unit costs will remain constant for variable costs. So if the unit variable cost is $5 per piece, it will remain the same even if the volume doubles. But in cases where raw materials can be procured cheaper in bulk and where economies of scale exist, unit variable cost could reduce. Similar effect can be seen if the volume decreases significantly and volume discounts can no longer be availed.

Secondly, unit costs of fixed costs reduce as the volume increases and increase with a reduction of volume because total fixed cost remains same irrespective of volume. Unit cost of total cost will almost always be misleading unless fixed costs are first removed. Below is an example.

Number of units: 1,000

Total Variable cost: $10,000

Total Fixed cost: $50,000

Hence, Unit Variable cost = $10,000 / 1,000 = $10

Unit Fixed cost = $50,000 / 1,000 = $50

Total Unit cost = $10 + $50 = $60

Now if the company produces 2,000 units instead of 1,000, then the unit costs will be as below:

Unit Variable cost = $10 (this will not change with number of units)

Unit Fixed cost = $50,000 / 2,000 = $25

Total Unit cost = $10 + $25 = $35

Total Variable cost = $10 * 2,000 = $20,000

In summary, unit costs should always be computed by first separating fixed costs from variable costs and keeping in mind the effect of volume discounts and economies of scale.

Inventoriable Costs

All costs related to manufacturing that can be inventorized into the company's balance sheet are called inventoriable costs. They fall under the following three categories:

a) Direct material costs – cost of materials required to make the product and whose cost can be traced back to the product

b) Direct manufacturing labor costs – cost of labor required to make the product and whose cost can be traced back to the product

c) Indirect manufacturing costs – these are the overhead costs that cannot be directly traced to the product but are related to the product

All inventoriable costs appear in the company's balance sheet under the item "Inventory" until the products are sold/ after which they appear in the company's income statement under the item "Cost of Goods Sold". Companies can have three types of inventory as below:

a) Direct materials inventory – inventory of raw materials

b) Work-in-process inventory – inventory of partially manufactured products

c) Finished goods inventory – inventory of ready products that are not yet sold

Consider an example of a pencil manufacturer. They have the following inventory levels:

Direct material (wood and lead) inventory: $500

Work-in-process inventory (including direct and indirect manufacturing costs): $2,000

Finished goods inventory (including direct and indirect manufacturing costs): $5,000

The company would show $7,500 ($500 + $2,000 + $5,000) as inventory in its balance sheet this year. If the company has managed to sell its entire finished goods inventory by next year and there is no other change then next year's balance sheet will show $2,500 ($500 + $2,000) as inventory and $5,000 will appear in the cost of goods sold in next year's income statement.

Period Costs

All costs that are not inventoriable are period costs. Examples are selling costs, marketing costs, R&D costs and distribution costs. These costs appear under expenses in the income statement. They are not part of cost of goods sold. They never appear in the balance sheet.

Prime Costs

These are all direct manufacturing costs. They are computed as given below:

Prime costs = Direct material costs + Direct manufacturing labor costs

Conversion Costs

These are the costs incurred in converting the raw materials into finished products. They are computed as given below:

Conversion costs = Direct manufacturing labor costs + Manufacturing overhead costs

Using a Costing System

A costing system is used primarily for two purposes – computing total cost incurred by a company, department or individual products/services and for making decisions using this data.

Cost Computation

As discussed earlier, every company has Direct and Indirect costs. Using these costs, companies compute Cost of Goods Sold (COGS), which is used for Financial Reporting via Income Statement (refer to chapter "Income Statement" in the book "Financial Accounting Essentials You Always Wanted to Know" of Self-Learning Management Series).

Below section shows how the costing data is used to compute Cost of Goods Manufactured, which is then used to compute

Cost of Goods Sold. Later chapters explain how Indirect costs are allocated using Activity Based Costing (ABC) and how Support Department costs are allocated.

Cost of Goods Manufactured

As the name suggests, Cost of Goods Manufactured is the cost incurred in manufacturing goods. It includes only inventoriable costs. Below diagram shows how it is computed:

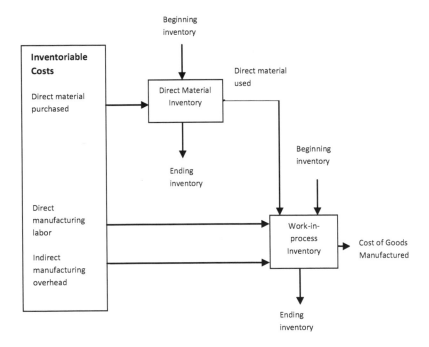

Consider the below example of how Cost of Goods Manufactured is computed using the above diagram. Following values are available for the year for a company:

a) Beginning inventory of Direct Materials = $500
b) Purchase of Direct Materials in the year = $200
c) Ending inventory of Direct Materials = $400
d) Beginning inventory of Work-in-process = $1,000
e) Ending inventory of Work-in-process = $900
f) Direct manufacturing labor for the year = $200
g) Indirect manufacturing overhead for the year = $100

Below are the computations for Cost of Goods Manufactured:

Direct Materials:		
Beginning inventory	$500	
Purchase of Direct Materials	$200	
Direct Materials available for use	$700	
Ending inventory	($400)	
Direct Materials used		$300
Direct Manufacturing Labor		$200
Indirect manufacturing overhead		$100
Manufacturing costs incurred		$600
Beginning Work-in-process inventory		$1,000
Total manufacturing costs to account for		$1,600
Ending Work-in-process inventory		($900)
Cost of Goods Manufactured		$700

Cost of Goods Sold

The item, Cost of Goods Sold, appears in the Income statement of those companies who have costs that are being reported as inventory until a sale takes place. Below diagram shows how it is calculated using Cost of Goods Manufactured:

Consider the example in the previous section. Below is some additional information that will help compute Cost of Goods Sold:

a) Beginning inventory of Finished goods = $400
b) Ending inventory of Finished goods = $600

Below is the computation of Cost of Goods Sold:

Beginning Finished goods inventory	$400
Cost of Goods Manufactured	$700
Cost of Goods available for sale	$1,100
Ending Finished goods inventory	($600)
Cost of Goods Sold	$500

Preparing the Income Statement

Income Statement contains Cost of Goods Sold and Period costs described above. Consider the example given in the previous section. Below are the revenue and period costs:

a) Revenue = $1,500

b) R&D cost = $100

c) Marketing cost = $200

d) Customer service cost = $150

Below is the Income Statement:

Revenue			$	1,500.00
Cost of Goods Sold			$	500.00
Gross Profit			$	1,000.00
Operating costs				
R&D	$	100.00		
Marketing	$	200.00		
Customer service	$	150.00		
Total operating costs			$	450.00
Operating Income			$	550.00

Note that as a convention we do not mention expenses as negative values in the Income Statement. Revenues are always added and expenses are always subtracted while computing Operating Income. With this knowledge it is much easier to read and understand income statements.

Decision Making

Costing systems are also used for decision making. In the next chapter we would see how costs affect volume and profit of the company. The later chapter shows how costing systems help in taking decisions using relevant information.

Solved Examples

1.1 A car manufacturer makes five different car models at its plant. Separate assembly lines are used for each model. Classify the various cost items given below into:
   a) Direct or Indirect
   b) Variable or Fixed

Answer with respect to any one car model.

   i.   Annual awards dinner for suppliers
   ii.   Fire insurance policy for the plant
   iii.   Cost of tires of the car model
   iv.   Salary of marketing manager of the plant
   v.   Salary of design engineer of the car model
   vi.   Freight costs of engines from foreign supplier
   vii.   Power bill for the entire plant
   viii. Hourly wages paid to temporary workers where each worker works on a single car model

Solution:

   i.   Annual awards dinner for suppliers – Indirect & Fixed
          This cost cannot be traced to any particular car model (assuming that suppliers supply parts for multiple car models and there is no clear separation between suppliers of a particular model) and does not vary with manufactured volumes.
   ii.   Fire insurance policy for the plant – Indirect & Fixed
          This also cannot be traced nor does it vary with volume.
   iii.   Cost of tires of the car model – Direct & Variable

This can be directly traced to the car and varies with the number of cars produced.

iv. Salary of marketing manager of the plant – Indirect & Fixed

The marketing manager is shared across all car models so the cost cannot be easily traced to one car model. It is also expected that changes in volume should not have any effect on the salary. In reality, however, the marketing manager could have bonus that is based on car sold or the company may add more managers if the volumes increase a lot. In both cases, the cost may still not be directly proportional to volume but will be more like a chunky step-cost.

v.   Salary of design engineer of the car model – Direct & Fixed

This cost can be directly traced to the particular car model and is not expected to vary proportionately with volume.

vi. Freight costs of engines from foreign supplier – Direct & Variable

This can be directly attributed to a single car model and has a direct relationship with volume as each car has one engine.

vii. Power bill for the entire plant – Indirect & Variable

Since there is a single power bill it cannot be traced to individual models but varies with volume of production.

viii. Hourly wages paid to temporary workers – Direct & Variable

Since each worker would work on a particular car model and they get hourly wages, the cost can be directly traced to the car and is directly proportional to number of cars manufactured.

1.2 Using the information given below for AAA Inc. compute the cost of goods manufactured and the income statement for the year. Also calculate prime and conversion costs.

Item	Beginning balance	Ending balance
Direct materials inventory	$10,000	$15,000
Work-in-process inventory	$20,000	$18,000
Finished goods inventory	$15,000	$20,000
Direct material purchases		$20,000
Direct manufacturing labor		$3,500
Indirect manufacturing labor		$2,500
Depreciation of plant		$2,000
Insurance of plant		$1,500
Plant maintenance costs		$3,000
Marketing costs		$5,000
Administrative costs		$2,000
Revenue		$50,000

Solution:

In the above information the following are inventoriable and period costs. The prior go in computation of cost of goods manufactured and the latter go in the income statement.

Item	Type of Cost
Direct material purchases	Inventoriable
Direct manufacturing labor	Inventoriable
Indirect manufacturing labor	Inventoriable
Depreciation of plant	Inventoriable
Insurance of plant	Inventoriable
Plant maintenance costs	Inventoriable
Marketing costs	Period
Administrative costs	Period

Below is the computation of cost of goods manufactured:

Direct Materials:		
Beginning inventory	$10,000	
Purchase of Direct Materials	$20,000	
Direct Materials available for use	$30,000	
Ending inventory	($15,000)	
Direct Materials used		$15,000
Direct Manufacturing Labor		$3,500
Overhead costs:		
Indirect manufacturing labor	$2,500	
Depreciation of plant	$2,000	
Insurance of plant	$1,500	
Plant maintenance costs	$3,000	
Indirect manufacturing overhead		$9,000
Manufacturing costs incurred		$27,500
Beginning Work-in-process inventory		$20,000
Total manufacturing costs to account for		$47,500
Ending Work-in-process inventory		($18,000)
Cost of Goods Manufactured		$29,500

Below is the computation of cost of goods sold:

Beginning Finished goods inventory	$15,000
Cost of Goods Manufactured	$29,500
Cost of Goods available for sale	$44,500
Ending Finished goods inventory	($20,000)
Cost of Goods Sold	$24,500

Below is the Income Statement:

Revenue		$ 50,000.00
Cost of Goods Sold		$ 24,500.00
Gross Profit		$ 25,500.00
Operating costs		
Marketing	$ 5,000.00	
Administrative	$ 2,000.00	
Total operating costs		$ 7,000.00
Operating Income		$ 18,500.00

Prime costs = Direct material costs + Direct manufacturing labor costs = $15,000 + $3,500 = $18,500

Conversion costs = Direct manufacturing labor costs + Manufacturing overhead costs = $3,500 + $9,000 = $12,500

Practice Exercises

1.1 A marketing research company organizes customer focus groups for its clients. Those who take part in the survey get paid by the hour for each session. The company has also hired professionals who organize and conduct these sessions. They are paid a fixed salary apart from a variable component for each session that they conduct. Classify the various cost items given below into:

    a) Direct or Indirect

    b) Variable or Fixed

Below are the costs to classify

   i.   Meals provided to participants during session

  ii.   Rent of company's corporate office

 iii.   Annual subscription charges of marketing research magazines

  iv.   Payment to participants of the session

   v.   Fixed amount paid to professionals who conduct the sessions

  vi.   Telecommunication cost paid in calling participants of focus groups

 vii.   Transportation costs of company's employees who travel for the session

1.2 Following is the information available on XYZ Inc.

Purchase of direct materials	$54,000
Indirect labor	$15,000
Direct labor	$31,200

Depreciation on machinery	$9,000
Sales	$165,900
Selling and administrative expenses	$18,900
Rent on factory building	$21,000

	Inventories	
	Beginning	Ending
Direct materials	$24,000	$26,100
Work-in-process	$6,300	$9,600
Finished goods	$15,000	$17,100

Using the above information prepare a statement of goods manufactured and income statement. Compute prime and conversion costs.

1.3 ZZZ Inc. designs office and residential buildings. Following data is available:

Direct Labor	$600,000
Direct material purchases	$40,000
Administrative costs	$130,000
Overhead costs	$75,000
Selling costs	$265,000
Beginning direct materials inventory	$20,000
Beginning designs in process	$14,000
Ending direct materials inventory	$10,000
Ending designs in process	$39,000

The average design fee is $700 and 2,000 designs were processed during the year.

Compute the cost of goods (designs) manufactured and prepare the income statement.

This page is intentionally left blank.

CHAPTER 2:

Cost-Volume-Profit (CVP) Analysis

A Cost-Volume-Profit (CVP) analysis examines the behaviour of total revenue, total costs, and operating income due to changes in units sold (volume), selling price, variable cost per unit, or fixed cost. This analysis helps make decisions related to selling price of a product or service, or choosing a cost structure from various cost structures that are available. We shall see its use later in this chapter.

Contribution Income Statement

This is a modified form of an Income Statement that is used in CVP analysis. Below diagram shows the difference:

Regular Income Statement		Contribution Income Statement		
Revenues	$ 1,000	Revenues		$ 1,000
Cost of goods sold	$ 500	Variable manufacturing costs	$ 200	
Gross profit	$ 500	Variable non-manufacturing costs	$ 100	$ 300
Non-manufacturing costs	$ 200	Contribution margin		$ 700
Operating Income	$ 300	Fixed manufacturing costs	$ 300	
		Fixed non-manufacturing costs	$ 100	$ 400
		Operating income		$ 300

As seen above, both income statements give the same operating income but the costs are re-arranged to provide different information. The fixed and variable costs are separately mentioned in the Contribution Income Statement to get the Contribution Margin.

Contribution Margin Equations

Operating Income = Revenues – Variable Costs – Fixed Costs

However, Revenues = Selling Price * Quantity Sold

& Variable Costs = Variable Cost per Unit * Quantity Sold

So, **Operating Income = (Selling Price * Quantity Sold) – (Variable Cost per Unit * Quantity Sold) – Fixed Costs**

In terms of Contribution Margin, the above equation can be written as:

Operating Income = (Contribution Margin per Unit * Quantity Sold) – Fixed Costs

Where, Contribution Margin per Unit = Selling Price – Variable Cost per Unit

Another important measure is the Contribution Margin Percentage given as:

Contribution Margin Percentage = Contribution Margin / Revenue

In the above example, Contribution Margin Percentage = $700 / $1,000 = 0.7 or 70%

CVP Analysis

As we stated earlier, this is the analysis of certain variables (revenue, cost, operating income) due to change in others (volume, variable cost per unit, fixed cost, selling price). Let's look at the effects one at a time.

Change in Volume

SP = $100	5 units sold		50 units sold	
Revenues	5 * 100	$500	50 * 100	$5,000
Variable costs	5 * 70	$350	50 * 70	$3,500
Fixed costs		$600		$600
Operating income		($450)		$900

Revenues and operating income change with a change in volume. Variable cost per unit and fixed cost remain the same. In the first case the company would incur a loss if it sold only five units. This is because the revenues are not enough to cover all the fixed costs.

Change in Selling Price

Volume = 15	SP = $100		SP = $120	
Revenues	15 * 100	$1,500	15 * 120	$1,800
Variable costs	15 * 70	$1,050	15 * 70	$1,050
Fixed costs		$600		$600
Operating income		($150)		$150

Revenues and operating income once again change with a change in the selling price. Other values remain constant. Once again there could be a loss if the selling price is too low to cover the fixed costs.

Change in Variable cost per Unit

Volume = 20, SP = $100	Var cost / unit = $80		Var cost / unit = $60	
Revenues	20 * 100	$2,000	20 * 100	$2,000
Variable costs	20 * 80	$1,600	20 * 60	$1,200
Fixed costs		$600		$600
Operating income		($200)		$200

Lower variable cost per unit has a favourable impact on the operating income but it does not change the revenues at fixed volume and selling price.

Change in Fixed Costs

Volume = 40, SP = $100	Fixed costs = $1,000		Fixed costs = $500	
Revenues	40 * 100	$4,000	40 * 100	$4,000
Variable costs	40 * 80	$3,200	40 * 80	$3,200
Fixed costs		$1,000		$500
Operating income		($200)		$300

Change in fixed costs affect operating income only. Everything else remains the same. Hence, fixed costs have a direct impact on the operating income and, are a very useful area to consider when trying to reduce costs.

Breakeven Point & Target Income

The point at which the total revenues are equal to the total costs is called Breakeven Point (BEP). At this point the operating income is equal to 0. Applying this to the contribution margin equation we get the following:

Operating Income = 0 = (Contribution Margin per Unit * Quantity Sold) – Fixed Costs

Hence, Quantity sold at BEP = Fixed Costs / Contribution Margin per Unit

If one needs to find out the quantity to be sold to achieve certain amount of operating income then we could do so using the equation below:

Quantity sold = (Operating Income + Fixed Costs) / Contribution Margin per Unit

Let's take an example. A company needs to find the breakeven point of one of its new products. Below are the available details:

Selling price = $100

Variable cost per unit = $65

Fixed costs = $20,000

We can compute the contribution margin per unit as below:

Contribution margin per unit = $100 - $65 = $35

At BEP, operating income = 0

Hence, Quantity sold at BEP = Fixed costs / Contribution margin per unit = $20,000 / $35 = 571.43

So the company needs to sell at least 572 units of the product to achieve breakeven.

Now assume, instead, that the company is looking to generate $5,000 from this product and wants to know how much it should sell. Below is the calculation:

Quantity sold = (Operating income + Fixed costs) / Contribution margin per unit

= ($5,000 + $20,000) / $35 = 714.3

Hence, the company needs to sell at least 715 units to achieve the desired operating income.

Tax Effect

If the company is looking for a target Net Income instead of Operating Income then the effect of tax needs to be considered as below:

Net Income = Operating Income * (1 – Tax rate)

Hence, **Operating Income = Net Income / (1 – Tax rate)**

Below is an example of calculating quantity sold at BEP to achieve a certain Net Income:

Selling Price = $200

Variable cost per unit = $100

Fixed costs = $25,000

Net Income = $20,000

Tax rate = 30%

Operating Income = Net Income / (1 – Tax rate) = $20,000 / (1 – 0.3) = $28,571.43

Contribution margin per unit = Selling Price – Variable cost per unit = $200 - $100 = $100

Quantity sold = (Operating income + Fixed costs) / Contribution margin per unit

= ($28,571.43 + $25,000) / $100 = 535.72

Hence, the company would need to sell at least 536 units to achieve the required net income.

CVP Analysis for Decision Making

As seen above CVP analysis is used to analyze effects of several variables on others. Below are some of the areas of decision making where this analysis helps:

Decision to Advertise

When a company needs to decide on whether it should advertise or not, it can turn to CVP analysis for the answer. The analysis would show whether advertising would increase operating income or not. If it does, then it is better to advertise. Otherwise, it is not. Let us take an example:

A company thinks that it can sell 100 units of a product in a convention if it does not advertise at all. However, if it does advertise, it expects to sell 150 units. The cost of advertising is $15,000. This adds to the other fixed costs of $5,000. Variable cost per unit, other fixed costs and selling price do not change. Below is a comparison of the two situations:

SP = $500, Var cost / unit = $300	Without advertising		With advertising	
Revenues	100 * 500	$50,000	150 * 500	$75,000
Variable costs	100 * 300	$30,000	150 * 300	$45,000
Contribution margin		$20,000		$30,000
Fixed costs		$5,000		$20,000
Operating Income		$15,000		$10,000

As seen from the above comparison, operating income with advertising is actually lower than it is without advertising. Hence, the company is better off selling lesser without advertising as the additional fixed cost of advertising is not being covered by the additional revenue generated.

Decision to Reduce Selling Price

If the company wants to increase its income by reducing the selling price so as to sell more units then again it can use CVP analysis to analyze this change. If the analysis shows that the operating income will increase by selling more units at a lower price, then that option would be preferable. Let us take an example.

A company can sell 1,000 units of a product at a selling price of $200 but if it reduces the selling price by 20% then it can sell 30% more units. The fixed costs would remain the same in both at $10,000. Variable cost per unit also remains constant at $100. Below is a comparison:

	SP = $200		SP = $160	
Revenues	1000 * 200	$200,000	1300 * 160	$208,000
Variable costs	1000 * 100	$100,000	1300 * 100	$130,000
Contribution margin		$100,000		$78,000
Fixed costs		$10,000		$10,000
Operating Income		$90,000		$68,000

Once again the company seems to be in a better position keeping the selling price at $200 as that gives higher operating income even though the volume is lower.

Decision to Select Cost Structure

When a company has choice of selecting one of many cost structures, it would choose the one that gives the most operating income. The cost structures would be different levels of fixed and variable costs. Let us take an example:

Let's say that a company is planning to keep a stall to sell its products in an electronics expo. The expo rents out stalls with the below alternative payment arrangements:

Alternative 1: $250,000 fixed charge

Alternative 2: $50,000 fixed charge + 2% of revenue earned at the stall

Alternative 3: No fixed charge but 10% of revenue earned at the stall

In order for the company to choose from the above alternatives it needs to do a CVP analysis with the following data:

Selling price = $500

Variable cost per unit = $150

Units sold (expected) = 10,000

	Alternative 1		Alternative 2		Alternative 3	
Revenues	10,000 * 500	$5,000,000	10,000 * 500	$5,000,000	10,000 * 500	$5,000,000
Variable costs	10,000 * 150	$1,500,000	10,000 * 150	$1,500,000	10,000 * 150	$1,500,000
Contribution margin		$3,500,000		$3,500,000		$3,500,000
Fixed costs		$250,000		$150,000		$500,000
Operating income		$3,250,000		$3,350,000		$3,000,000

From the above analysis it is clear that Alternative 2 is the one that would bring the most income to the company and so it should select that option.

The above example has alternatives that differ only in the fixed costs. Degree of Operating Leverage can be used to see the effects of fixed costs on operating income for different units of product sold and contribution margin as given below:

Degree of Operating Leverage = Contribution Margin / Operating Income

Applying it to the above example gives the following:

	Alternative 1		Alternative 2		Alternative 3	
Revenues	10,000 * 500	$5,000,000	10,000 * 500	$5,000,000	10,000 * 500	$5,000,000
Variable costs	10,000 * 150	$1,500,000	10,000 * 150	$1,500,000	10,000 * 150	$1,500,000
Contribution margin		$3,500,000		$3,500,000		$3,500,000
Fixed costs		$250,000		$150,000		$500,000
Operating income		$3,250,000		$3,350,000		$3,000,000
Operating Leverage		1.08		1.04		1.17

As seen above, the Operating Leverage is lowest for Alternative 2 which has the least fixed cost and highest for Alternative 3 which has the highest fixed cost. Operating leverage is the percentage by which the operating income would change for a 1% change in the revenue or contribution margin. Below is how it can be used:

For Alternative 3, a 1% change in revenue would be:

Revenues = $5,000,000 + $50,000 = $5,050,000

This will be for Units = $5,050,000 / $500 = 10,100

Below are the calculations:

	Alternative 3	
Revenues	10,100 * 500	$5,050,000
Variable costs	10,100 * 150	$1,515,000
Contribution margin		$3,535,000
Fixed costs		$500,000
Operating income		$3,035,000

Change in Operating Income = $3,035,000 - $3,000,000 = $35,000

Percentage change in Operating Income = $35,000 / $3,000,000 = 0.0117 or 1.17%

When fixed costs are higher, the degree of Operating Leverage is also higher. This gives greater incentive to companies to increase their revenues as it adds a greater percentage to the operating income. Having a high degree of operating leverage is neither good nor bad. In most cases it depends on the industry's typical cost structure. For example/ power generation companies have high fixed costs due to huge capital investment and hence have a higher degree of Operating Leverage. Services companies have a much lower fixed cost and hence lower degree of Operating Leverage.

Sensitivity Analysis

Knowing that the company would make a profit may sometimes not be enough as there could be uncertainty in the number of units sold. It might also be useful to know how much risk the company is running of making a loss. This is measured by Margin of Safety, given below:

Margin of Safety = Budgeted revenues – Breakeven revenues

Margin of Safety (in units) = Budgeted sales (in units) – Breakeven sales (in units)

It is also represented in percentage form as below:

Margin of Safety Percentage = Margin of safety / Budgeted revenues

Margin of Safety Percentage gives the percentage by which the revenues should fall in order for the company to start making losses. Below is an example:

Selling Price = $50

Variable costs per Unit = $20

Fixed costs = $20,000

Budgeted units sold = 1,000

Below is the calculation for BEP:

BEP units = Fixed Costs / Contribution Margin per Unit = $20,000 / ($50 - $20) = 667 units

BEP revenues = $50 * 667 = $33,350

Budgeted revenues = $50 * 1,000 = $50,000

Therefore, Margin of Safety = $50,000 - $33,350 = $16,650

Margin of Safety (in units) = 1,000 – 667 = 333 units

Margin of Safety Percentage = $16,650 / $50,000 = 33.3%

This means that the revenue needs to fall 33.3% for the company to start making losses. This looks like a good margin of safety.

Solved Examples

2.1 **AAA Inc. manufactures ball pens. It sold 50,000 units last year, each for $20. Variable costs per unit are $11 and total fixed costs are $200,000.**

a) **Calculate contribution margin and operating income.**

b) **The company is planning to buy a new machine that would reduce the variable cost to $8 but it will cost $100,000 to procure and install. How does this change the contribution margin and operating income?**

c) **Should the new machine be bought?**

Solution:

a) Below sheet shows the contribution margin and operating income:

Revenues	50,000 * 20	$1,000,000
Variable costs	50,000 * 11	$550,000
Contribution margin		$450,000
Fixed costs		$200,000
Operating Income		$250,000

b) Below sheet shows the calculations based on the new machine:

Revenues	50,000 * 20	$1,000,000
Variable costs	50,000 * 8	$400,000
Contribution margin		$600,000
Fixed costs		$300,000
Operating Income		$300,000

c) As seen from the above calculations, the Operating Income increases with the new machine. Hence the company should buy the new machine.

2.2 XYZ Inc. sells airline tickets at a rate of $500 per ticket from LA to San Francisco. It gets a 20% commission on each ticket sold and incurs $10 variable cost in delivering the tickets to customers. It also has a fixed cost of $100,000 per year.

a) Determine how many tickets the company will need to sell to achieve breakeven.

b) How many more tickets does it need to sell to get an Operating Income of $250,000?

Solution:

Selling Price = $100 (only 20% of ticket price is the company's revenue)

Variable cost per ticket = $10

Fixed costs = $100,000

Contribution margin per ticket = $100 - $10 = $90

a) Number of tickets at BEP = Fixed costs / Contribution margin per ticket = $100,000 / $90 = 1,112

b) Number of tickets to get Operating Income = (Fixed costs + Operating Income) / Contribution margin per ticket

= ($100,000 + $250,000) / $90 = 3,889

HARRISON COLLEGE
Indianapolis Downtown

2.3 ZZZ Inc. has decided to sell chairs in an exhibition. It will sell each chair at $1,000 which is procured at $700 from a local vendor in bulk. The vendor has agreed to take back any chairs which are not sold. However, he will charge a $10,000 fixed fee for doing so. The company estimates that 100 chairs will be sold.

a) Calculate Operating Income.

b) What is the Degree of Operating Leverage when selling 100 chairs?

c) How much will Operating Income change if revenue increases by 1%?

Solution:

a) Below is the calculation of Operating Income:

Revenues	100 * 1,000	$100,000
Variable costs	100 * 700	$70,000
Contribution margin		$30,000
Fixed costs		$10,000
Operating Income		$20,000

b) Degree of Operating Leverage = Contribution Margin / Operating Income
= $30,000 / $20,000 = 1.5

c) Since the degree of operating leverage is 1.5, 1% increase in revenue will increase the operating income by 1.5%.

Practice Exercises

2.1 Following information is given:
   Variable Costs = $5,000
   Operating Income = $2,000
   Contribution Margin = $4,000

   Calculate:
   a) Revenues
   b) Fixed Costs
   c) Contribution Margin Percentage

2.2 AAA Inc. sells vases for $4 each. Following is its cost structure:
   Variable costs per unit –

Direct materials	$0.6
Direct labor	$0.8
Factory overhead	$0.5
Administrative	$0.3

   Fixed costs –

Overheads	$9,000
Marketing	$5,000

   The company sells 10,000 vases during the year.

   Determine the following:
   a) What is the company's breakeven point (BEP)?

b) If sales increase by 500 vases, what will be the change in profit?

c) If the tax rate is 40%, how much sales are required for a Net Income of $12,000?

2.3 ZZZ Inc. has the following Contribution Income Statement for the year:

Sales	$25,000
Variable expenses	$15,000
Contribution Margin	$10,000
Fixed expenses	$4,000
Operating Income	$6,000

a) Calculate degree of operating leverage

b) If sales increase by 20%, what will be the percentage change in income?

2.4 XYZ Inc. is planning to rent a place temporarily for selling apparels. It expects to do business only for a month when several tourists are expected due to football matches in the city. It has got two options for renting.

Option 1: Fixed rent of $35,000
Option 2: Fixed rent of 10,000 + 5% of sales revenue

Below data is also available:

Average selling price of apparel = $50

Expected volumes to sell = 5,000

Variable cost per apparel = $20

Fixed costs of personnel = $5,000

a) What is the Operating Income for each option?

b) Which is a better option to take?

CHAPTER 3:

Decision Making using Relevant Information

When decisions are being made about outsourcing, product-mix or one-time orders, not all costs are relevant. Managers make such decisions only using the relevant costs. For example, generally the fixed costs do not change across alternatives and, hence, most often they are not considered while taking a decision. Costs and revenue are called relevant only when they meet the two criteria below:

a) *Occur in future* – only future costs and revenue are relevant. Past costs are called sunk costs and are never relevant in decision making as they cannot be recovered. Same is the case with past revenue.

b) *Differ among alternatives* – only those costs that are different among alternatives are considered for decision making. As stated above, generally the fixed costs do not change among alternatives, and, hence are not relevant.

Consider an example where a company is considering reorganization, wherein, it would need to lay off some workers. The reorganization itself would have a cost. The sheet below shows all the costs of both the alternatives along with a difference showing the relevant costs.

	Alternative 1 Do not Reorganize		Alternative 2 Reorganize	Difference Relevant costs
Revenues		$100,000	$100,000	$0
Costs:				
Direct materials	$20,000		$20,000	$0
Direct labor	$30,000		$20,000	($10,000)
Manufacturing overhead	$10,000		$10,000	$0
Marketing	$15,000		$15,000	$0
Reorganization cost	$0		$5,000	$5,000
Total costs		$75,000	$70,000	($5,000)
Operating Income		$25,000	$30,000	$5,000

In the above sheet, revenues and most of the costs of both alternatives are the same. The only difference is in the Direct labor and Reorganization costs. This is because due to reduction in workers, the labor cost goes down and reorganization cost gets added. The difference shows that these two are the only relevant items to consider in making this decision. It is quite obvious that Alternative 2 should be selected as it has a higher Operating Income. This decision is purely based on quantitative factors. But the reorganization would lead to layoffs that could reduce employee morale. This is one of the qualitative factors to consider.

The next few sections describe different scenarios of short-term tactical decision making using relevant information.

One-Time-Only Special Orders

When a company gets a one-time order from a customer while it has got idle capacity, the company would use relevant information to decide whether to accept the offer or not. It has to be assumed that this order would not make any long-term difference to the company's business/ like other customers asking for a discount or affecting the selling price of other customers. The one-time order needs to be a special order that is not expected to recur or have any long-term impact on the company's regular business.

Quantitative Factors

Let's assume that a company making hot plates has a capacity of making 20,000 units but is currently making only 15,000 units for its customers. It receives a one-time-only order from a hotel chain to provide 5,000 hot plates at $425 each. The regular price is $800 per hot plate. The variable costs are as below:

Direct materials cost = $350

Direct labor cost = $50

Variable Marketing costs = $50

The fixed costs are as below:

Fixed Manufacturing costs = $200,000

Fixed marketing costs = $500,000

The variable marketing cost is not expected to increase due to the special order.

The below sheet shows the company's income statement without the special order:

		Total	Per Unit
Revenues		$12,000,000	$800
Variable costs:			
Direct materials	$5,250,000		$350
Direct labor	$750,000		$50
Marketing	$750,000		$50
Total Variable costs		$6,750,000	
Contribution Margin		$5,250,000	
Fixed costs:			
Manufacturing	$200,000		
Marketing	$500,000		
Total Fixed costs:		$700,000	
Operating Income		$4,550,000	

Now if the company accepts the special order then the company's income statement would look like below. It gives both the income statements for side-by-side comparison. The last column gives only the relevant costs.

		Without Special Order		With Special Order		Relevant Costs
		Total	Per Unit	Total	Per Unit	
Revenues		$12,000,000	$800	$14,125,000	$425	$2,125,000
Variable costs:						
Direct materials	$5,250,000		$350	$7,000,000	$350	($1,750,000)
Direct labor	$750,000		$50	$1,000,000	$50	($250,000)
Marketing	$750,000		$50	$750,000	$50	$0
Total Variable costs		$6,750,000		$8,750,000		($2,000,000)
Contribution Margin		$5,250,000		$5,375,000		$125,000
Fixed costs:						
Manufacturing	$200,000			$200,000		$0
Marketing	$500,000			$500,000		$0
Total Fixed costs:		$700,000		$700,000		$0
Operating Income		$4,550,000		$4,675,000		$125,000

The relevant costs are only the additional revenue (5,000 * $425), Direct materials and Direct labor costs. Variable Marketing costs are staying constant when accepting the special order and so are all the Fixed costs. Even though the selling price of the special order is much lower than the regular selling price, the company is still able to increase its operating income by accepting the order. Hence, managers taking decision based on quantitative factors only would accept the special order.

Qualitative Factors

Following qualitative factors might also be taken into account before taking a decision. These are more long-term and strategic in nature.

a) When companies take one-time-only special orders, they need to ensure that other customers do not ask for that price as it would reduce their profit margin from regular business

b) Special orders could lead to over time and reduce employee morale

Make-or-Buy Decisions

When companies need to decide whether to make certain parts themselves or to outsource them, once again, they turn to cost accounting for a quantitative analysis.

Quantitative Factors

Below are the costs of manufacturing a part required in the company's cars0

Direct material costs = $100,000

Direct manufacturing labor = $200,000

Variable manufacturing overheads (setup, utility costs) = $40,000

Fixed manufacturing overheads (lease, rent, insurance costs) = $50,000

They produce 100,000 units of the part. Below is the total cost of manufacturing the part:

	Total	Per Unit
Direct materials	$100,000	$1.00
Direct manufacturing labor	$200,000	$2.00
Variable manufacturing overheads	$40,000	$0.40
Fixed manufacturing overheads	$50,000	$0.50
Total manufacturing costs	$390,000	$3.90

As seen above, the company incurs $3.9 per part when producing it. Another company offers to sell the same part to the company for $3.6. The company needs to decide whether to outsource production or not. Just looking at the above calculation, it may look like outsourcing is cheaper. But in order to take the decision, only relevant costs should be taken into account as below:

	Make		Buy	
	Total	Per Unit	Total	Per Unit
Procurement cost			$360,000	$3.60
Direct materials	$100,000	$1.00		
Direct manufacturing labor	$200,000	$2.00		
Variable manufacturing overheads	$40,000	$0.40		
Total relevant costs	$340,000	$3.40	$360,000	$3.60

In the above analysis, we have omitted the Fixed manufacturing overheads, as they are expected to stay even though the work is outsourced. The only relevant costs are the variable costs in this case. Hence, the company is better off making the part.

Qualitative Factors

Following qualitative factors could apply to make-or-buy decisions:

a) Companies might decide to make instead of buy to retain control over production even though outsourcing is cheaper.

b) Companies may prefer to outsource even though it is costlier in order to concentrate on their core competencies. This means that outsourcing could be costlier but the company would like to concentrate on other areas of business that could add value in future.

c) Outsourcing decision may not always be based on cost. Companies look at quality of product and try to maintain long-term relationship with suppliers to avoid delays in delivery schedule.

Outsourcing and Opportunity Costs

In the above example the company decides not to go for outsourcing with an assumption that the released capacity would not be used for any other purpose. However, if the company is able to rent out the premises to someone else or use the capacity to manufacture something else, then that additional revenue needs to be considered before taking a decision based on the quantitative analysis. The cost associated with the lost opportunity of using the premises for some other purpose is called Opportunity Cost.

Let's say that in the above example/ the company is able to rent out its premises to another company for a rent of $70,000. This amount is called opportunity cost. It is the loss of revenue or opportunity of selecting an alternative. This amount can be either subtracted from total costs of alternative 2 or added to total costs of alternative 1. We shall add it to the total costs of alternative 1. Then the analysis would look like below:

	Make		Buy	
	Total	Per Unit	Total	Per Unit
Procurement cost			$360,000	$3.60
Opportunity cost (of renting)	$70,000	$0.70		
Direct materials	$100,000	$1.00		
Direct manufacturing labor	$200,000	$2.00		
Variable manufacturing overheads	$40,000	$0.40		
Total relevant costs	$410,000	$4.10	$360,000	$3.60

Now from the above analysis it is clear that the alternative to buy from outside is better. Similarly, consider that the company is able to use the premises for producing something else rather than renting. The incremental revenues and costs would be as below:

	Total
Incremental Revenues	$500,000
Incremental Costs	$400,000
Incremental Operating Income	$100,000

The new part that is produced will bring incremental revenue of $500,000 at an additional incremental cost of $400,000. This gives an incremental operating income of $100,000. Below is the comparison of the two alternatives now:

	Make		Buy	
	Total	Per Unit	Total	Per Unit
Procurement cost			$360,000	$3.60
Opportunity cost (of making other part)	$100,000	$1.00		
Direct materials	$100,000	$1.00		
Direct manufacturing labor	$200,000	$2.00		
Variable manufacturing overheads	$40,000	$0.40		
Total relevant costs	$440,000	$4.40	$360,000	$3.60

Product-Mix Decisions with Capacity Constraints

Most companies produce more than one product or service. They may also have constraints in their production. For example, if a company makes two different car models using the same assembly line, the assembly line would become a constraint if it is unable to produce enough units that can be sold. Hence, they need to decide on the product-mix to produce. The capacity does not allow the companies to produce everything they can sell. They need to select the product-mix that maximizes their operating income. Shown below is an example of a company producing two products:

	Product 1	Product 2
Selling Price	$100	$120
Variable cost per unit	$70	$76
Contribution margin per unit	$30	$44
Contribution margin percentage	30.00%	36.67%

Simply looking at the above information the company might decide to produce only Product 2. But due to capacity constraints, the company also needs to look at how much of the capacity constrained resource is being used by the two products before deciding. Below is the information of how much each product uses the machine that has constrained capacity:

	Product 1	Product 2
Contribution margin per unit	$30	$44
Machine hours on capacity constrained machine	2	4
Contribution margin per machine hour	$15	$11

From the above analysis it is clear that more number of Product 1 can be produced by the company and that gives the company greater contribution margin. Hence, it should produce more of Product 1.

Solved Examples

3.1 XYZ Inc. has got a proposal from its mechanical department to replace an old machine. Following data is available related to the current and new machines:

	Current machine	New machine
Original cost	$2,000,000	$900,000
Useful Life (in years)	5	3
Used Life (in years)	2	0
Accumulated depreciation	$800,000	$0
Current disposal value	$600,000	$0
Terminal disposal value (after 3 years)	$0	$0
Annual operating costs	$100,000	$50,000
Annual maintenance costs	$40,000	$40,000
Annual revenues	$2,000,000	$2,000,000

Should the company replace the current machine?

Solution:

In order to decide between the two alternatives, the company needs to calculate the operating income of the two alternatives. However, if only one year's operating income is taken into account then the analysis would be incomplete. Instead, operating income over three years (life of the new machine / useful life of the current machine is three years) should be taken into account. Below is the analysis:

Analysis for 3 years	Alternative 1 No replacement		Alternative 2 Do replacement	
Revenues	$2,000,000 * 3	$6,000,000	$2,000,000 * 3	$6,000,000
Costs:				
Operating costs	$100,000 * 3	$300,000	$50,000 * 3	$150,000
Maintenance costs	$40,000 * 3	$120,000	$40,000 * 3	$120,000
Remaining Depreciation	$2,000,000 - $800,000	$1,200,000	Full cost of machine	$900,000
Current disposal value	This is not a cost		Will reduce the cost	($600,000)
Terminal disposal value		$0		$0
Total costs		$1,620,000		$570,000
Operating Income		$4,380,000		$5,430,000

The Operating Income over three years from Alternative 2 is higher than Alternative 1. Hence, Alternative 2 should be selected.

3.2 ZZZ Inc. produces notebooks. They have capacity to produce 10,000 each month. Their current sales are 8,000. Their price per notebook is $50. Below are their current costs:

Direct materials	$80,000
Direct manufacturing labor	$40,000
Variable manufacturing costs	$40,000
Fixed manufacturing labor	$60,000
Fixed marketing costs	$25,000

Another company urgently needs 2,000 notebooks and asks ZZZ Inc. to sell them at $25 per notebook. This is a one-time-only special order without any long-term consequences. Should ZZZ Inc. accept the offer?

Solution:

The company has two alternatives. First one is to not accept the special order and the other one is to accept the offer at $25 per piece. Below is the analysis of each alternative:

	Without Special order		With Special order
	Total	Per Unit	Total
Revenues	$400,000	$50	$450,000
Variable Costs:			
Direct materials	$80,000	$10	$100,000
Direct manufacturing labor	$40,000	$5	$50,000
Variable manufacturing costs	$40,000	$5	$50,000
Contribution margin	$240,000	$30	$250,000
Fixed Costs:			
Fixed manufacturing labor	$60,000		$60,000
Fixed marketing costs	$25,000		$25,000
Operating Income	$155,000		$165,000

From the above analysis we find that the company can get higher Operating Income by accepting the special order.

3.3 AAA Inc. makes two products – P1 & P2. The following are prices and costs of the two products:

	P1	P2
Selling Price	$50	$20
Costs:		
Direct material	$10	$5
Direct labor	$7	$2
Variable manufacturing	$5	$1
Fixed manufacturing	$5	$2
Fixed marketing	$8	$3
Total Costs	$35	$13
Operating Income	$15	$7

It is further known that the company produces both the products using the same production process that is unable to produce as much as the sales of both products. Hence, the company needs to decide which product to produce more of. P1 takes 1 hour of the production process, whereas, P2 takes 20 minutes of the process. Which product should the company choose to produce?

Solution:

The company is having a capacity constraint – the production process. The company should not choose operating income as the criteria to select the product to produce. It should choose the contribution margin per hour of the production process to decide as fixed costs are irrelevant in decision making (they are going to be same for both alternatives). Below is the calculation:

	P1	P2
Selling Price	$50	$20
Variable Costs:		
Direct material	$10	$5
Direct labor	$7	$2
Variable manufacturing	$5	$1
Total Variable costs	$22	$8
Contribution margin	$28	$12
Use of production process (in hours)	1.00	0.33
Contribution margin per hour of constrained resource	$28	$36

As seen above, even though the contribution margin of P2 is much lower, its contribution margin per hour of the production process (the constraint) is much higher than P1. Hence, the company should produce only P2 as long as they can sell all that they produce. Any time left of the production process can then be devoted to producing P1.

Practice Exercises

3.1 Which of the following costs are relevant for decision making when there are two alternatives?
   a) Cost of equipment that is bought in Alternative 2
   b) Operating costs that are same for Alternatives 1 & 2
   c) Cost of equipment bought last year
   d) Fixed costs that will be incurred
   e) Depreciation of equipment that is kept in Alternative 1 and sold in Alternative 2

3.2 AAA Inc. currently buys 30,000 units of a part used to manufacture its product at $40 per unit. Recently the supplier informed that a 20% increase will take effect next year. AAA has some additional space and could produce the units for the following per unit costs:

Direct materials	$16
Direct labor	$12
Variable overhead	$12
Fixed overhead (based on 30,000 units)	$10

If the units are purchased from the supplier, $200,000 of fixed costs will still be incurred. In addition, the plant can be rented out for $20,000 per year if the parts are purchased externally.
Should the company buy the parts or make them?

3.3 XYZ Inc. manufactures a product with the following unit costs for 5,000 units:

Direct materials	$60
Direct labor	$30
Factory overhead (40% variable)	$90
Selling expenses (60% variable)	$30
Administrative expenses (20% variable)	$15

Recently a company approached XYZ Inc. to buy 1,000 units of the product for $225. Currently, it is sold for $412.50 to dealers. XYZ Inc. has enough capacity to produce the extra units. No additional selling expenses would be incurred on the special order.

a) Calculate the profit currently earned by the company
b) Should the company accept the special order?

This page is intentionally left blank.

CHAPTER 4:

Activity Based Costing

All companies have Direct and Indirect costs. Companies having only one product or service can allocate all indirect costs to it. However, companies having multiple products or services would need to allocate such costs on some basis. In this chapter we would see how indirect costs are allocated to products using individual activities instead of simple averaging.

Broad Averaging

Companies may decide to simply allocate all costs by averaging them across products. This approach leads to inaccurate costing and may result into product under-costing or product over-costing.

For example, consider four friends going out for dinner. They incur the following costs:

	Bob	Peter	Lisa	Julie	Total	Average
Starters	$10	$5	$2	$0	$17	$4.25
Main course	$20	$35	$30	$25	$110	$27.50
Drinks	$5	$15	$10	$10	$40	$10
Dessert	$0	$5	$10	$8	$23	$5.75
Total	$35	$60	$52	$43	$190	$47.50

Now if the friends decide to split the bill based on the broad average of $47.50, then Bob and Julie would be paying more than they should, whereas, Peter and Lisa would pay less. Now this might not be such a bad thing if they are close friends but it could lead to incorrect decisions in a company. Companies might take incorrect pricing decisions that are based on broad averages and may even decide to continue or discontinue the wrong product line or service. Such a situation is called product-cost cross-subsidization.

Simple Costing System

A simple costing system is based on above described broad averaging of costs. All indirect costs are allocated to a single indirect-cost pool and then allocated to the cost object using a single cost-allocation base. This is shown in the diagram below:

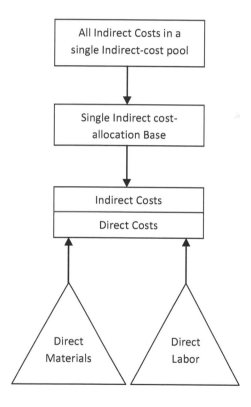

The selection of cost-allocation base is on some direct parameter, like direct manufacturing labor hours, total direct manufacturing costs etc. Once that is selected, all indirect costs are allocated using that base to all products or services (the cost objects). All direct costs are traced directly to the cost objects.

Consider the example of a company that manufactures CD players for cars. It has two models, CD2005 & CD2010. CD2005 is a plain old CD player and is cheaper. CD2010 is a new breed of CD players that can play multiple formats – audio CD, MP3 etc. The company sells these two players to a car manufacturer for $50 and $120 per player respectively. The car manufacturer has recently said that there is another company that is able to provide players of type CD2005 at $40. Hence, the company now needs to decide whether to reduce the price of its CD2005 player or discontinue selling that model if it is unable to match the cost structure of the competitor. Luckily, it does not have too much competition in CD2010 market right now.

The company sells 50,000 pieces of CD2005 and 20,000 pieces of CD2010 per year. Its total indirect costs are $1,000,000. It decides to use direct manufacturing labor hours as the cost-allocation base to allocate the indirect costs to the two cost objects – CD2005 & CD2010. The direct manufacturing labor hours for CD2005 are 15,000 and that of CD2010 are 10,000. Hence, the indirect cost per cost-allocation base (direct manufacturing labor hour) is:

Indirect cost per direct manufacturing labor hour = $1,000,000 / 25,000 = $40

Further assume the following:

Direct materials cost for producing 50,000 CD2005 = $1,000,000

Direct materials cost for producing 20,000 CD2010 = $1,000,000

Direct manufacturing labor cost for producing 50,000 CD2005 = $400,000

Direct manufacturing labor cost for producing 20,000 CD2010 = $200,000

Below are the cost calculations for both products:

	CD2005		CD2010	
	Total	Per Unit	Total	Per Unit
Direct materials	$1,000,000	$20.00	$1,000,000	$50.00
Direct manufacturing labor	$400,000	$8.00	$200,000	$10.00
Total direct costs	$1,400,000.00	$28.00	$1,200,000.00	$60.00
Indirect cost allocated ($40*15,000, $40*10,000)	$600,000	$12.00	$400,000	$20.00
Total cost	$2,000,000.00	$40.00	$1,600,000.00	$80.00
Selling Price		$50.00		$120.00
Operating margin		20%		33%

The company has done the allocation as per the diagram below:

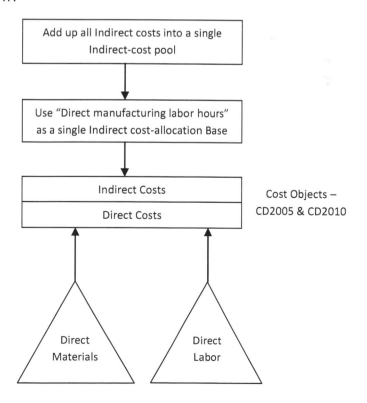

Decision Making

As seen from the above calculations, the company has a lower margin in CD2005 and higher in CD2010. By looking at this information the company may think that it is not profitable to sell CD2005 for $40 and might decide to forego that business and concentrate on the more profitable product – CD2010.

Activity Based Costing System

Activity Based Costing (ABC) is a system in which all indirect costs are first put into different pools based on the activities performed for the cost being incurred. In the next stage, each indirect-cost pool is allocated to the cost objects using its own indirect cost-allocation base. In effect, it has two differences compared to simple costing system as below:

a) Indirect costs are put in separate pools of activities
b) Allocation of indirect costs is done using separate cost-allocation bases

Below is the diagram showing an ABC system:

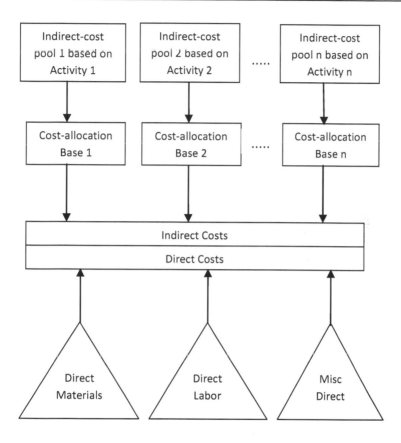

Apart from the multiple indirect cost-pools and cost-allocation bases, an ABC system also attempts to try and identify those costs that may seem indirect but are incurred only on a single product or service. In such cases they can be directly traced back to the cost object and they become a direct cost. Such costs are shown in the diagram as "Misc Direct".

Let's use the ABC system to analyze the cost structure of the company making CD2005 & CD2010 in the above example. But in order to do so, we need additional information on how the indirect costs are incurred – using which activities. The following information is available:

Activity	Budgeted Cost	Cost-allocation Base	Budgeted Quantity of cost-allocation Base	Indirect Cost Rate
Machine setup	$200,000	Direct	-	-
Distribution	$150,000	CD volume	200	$750
Design	$500,000	CD size	500	$1,000
Administration	$150,000	Direct manufacturing labor hours	25,000	$6
Total	$1,000,000			

The total indirect cost is divided into four activities. Machine setup is an activity that can be directly traced back to the particular CD model as they use different machines. Hence, it has been converted to a direct cost. Distribution activity can be allocated using the volume of CD as the volume determines the amount it takes to deliver. Design activity has CD size as the cost-allocation base as bigger size takes more design effort. Finally, administration is best allocated using direct manufacturing labor hours. Below sheet shows the costs using ABC:

	CD2005		CD2010	
	Total	Per Unit	Total	Per Unit
Direct materials	$1,000,000	$20.00	$1,000,000	$50.00
Direct manufacturing labor	$400,000	$8.00	$200,000	$10.00
Machine setup				
(direct cost based on number of setups)	$50,000	$1.00	$150,000	$7.50
Total direct costs	$1,450,000.00	$29.00	$1,350,000.00	$67.50
Distribution				
CD2005 - $750 * 50 cubic feet volume	$37,500.00	$0.75		
CD2010 - $750 * 150 cubic feet volume			$112,500.00	$5.63
Design				
CD2005 - $1,000 * 180 sq. feet	$180,000.00	$3.60		
CD2010 - $1,000 * 320 sq. feet			$320,000.00	$16.00
Administration				
CD2005 - $6 * 15,000 hr	$90,000	$1.80		
CD2010 - $6 * 10,000 hr			$60,000	$3.00
Total cost	$1,757,500.00	$35.15	$1,842,500.00	$92.13
Selling Price		$50.00		$120.00
Operating margin		30%		23%

The company has done the allocation as per the diagram below:

Decision Making

When the costs are allocated using ABC, it turns out that CD2005 is actually more profitable than CD2010. Even if the company wants to reduce the selling price to $40 for meeting the competitor's price/ it will still make a profit.

Customer Profitability

Activity-based costing is very useful in analyzing customer profitability. It is the difference between the revenues earned from a customer and the costs incurred in serving the customer. Several times companies are unaware of their most profitable customers and their least profitable ones or even loss making accounts. With this knowledge the company can decide how much effort it should put on which account in order to increase the overall profitability of the company.

Consider a company having four customers with the below customer revenues:

	Customers			
	A	B	C	D
Products sold	40,000	30,000	3,000	2,000
Listed selling price	$150	$150	$150	$150
Discount	$10	$5	$12	$0
Invoicing price	$140	$145	$138	$150
Cost of goods sold	$120	$120	$120	$120

If the company wants to find which of the above four customers are most and least profitable, it also needs to know the indirect costs associated with each of them. Below table gives this information on basis of an activity-based accounting system:

Activity	Rate	Cost driver
Storage	$5	Per product sold
Order handling	$500	Per purchase order
Delivery	$10	Per mile of delivery
Urgent delivery	$2,000	Per urgent delivery, irrespective of distance travelled
Sales cost	$1,000	Per salesperson visit

Below are the actual usages of the above activities per customer:

	Customers			
	A	B	C	D
Number of Purchase Orders	30	20	15	10
Number of deliveries	50	20	20	10
Average miles per delivery	10	10	20	5
Number of urgent deliveries	2	1	2	0
Number of salesperson visits	5	5	3	2

Using the above information the company can compute how much cost is associated with each customer and compute the customer profitability as below:

	Customers			
	A	B	C	D
Revenues				
$140 * 40,000				
$145 * 30,000				
$138 * 3,000				
$150 * 2,000	$5,600,000	$4,350,000	$414,000	$300,000
Cost of goods sold				
$120 * 40,000				
$120 * 30,000				
$120 * 3,000				
$120 * 2,000	$4,800,000	$3,600,000	$360,000	$240,000
Gross margin	$800,000	$750,000	$54,000	$60,000
Storage costs				
$5 * 40,000				
$5 * 30,000				
$5 * 3,000				
$5 * 2,000	$200,000	$150,000	$15,000	$10,000
Order handling costs				
$500 * 30				
$500 * 20				
$500 * 15				
$500 * 10	$15,000	$10,000	$7,500	$5,000
Delivery costs				
$10 * 50 * 10				
$10 * 20 * 10				
$10 * 20 * 20				
$10 * 10 * 5	$5,000	$2,000	$4,000	$500
Urgent delivery costs				
$2,000 * 2				
$2,000 * 1				
$2,000 * 2				
$2,000 * 0	$4,000	$2,000	$4,000	$0
Salesperson costs				
$1,000 * 5				
$1,000 * 5				
$1,000 * 3				
$1,000 * 2	$5,000	$5,000	$3,000	$2,000
Total indirect costs	$229,000	$169,000	$33,500	$17,500
Operating Income	$571,000	$581,000	$20,500	$42,500
Operating margin	10.20%	13.36%	4.95%	14.17%

As seen from the above analysis, customer D is the most profitable and customer C is least profitable. This is because the indirect costs of customer C are too high for the volume of business it gives to the company. Using this information the company can focus on customers B & D as they are the most profitable and reduce costs in serving customers C & A.

Solved Examples

4.1 AAA Inc. makes two types of bikes – regular and premium. Each bike has its own distribution channel. The total cost of distribution is $4,260,000. Below are some other details that are available:

Type	Number of Distributors	Number of Bikes
Regular	10	240,000
Premium	30	160,000

Currently the company allocates distribution costs on the basis of number of bikes shipped. In order to better understand its costs, the company identifies the following activities and related costs:

  i.   Marketing costs - $16,000 per distributor
  ii.   Order handling costs - $600 per order. A distributor of regular bikes places on average 10 orders per year and that of premium places 20 orders per year.
  iii. Delivery costs - $8 per bike

a) Calculate the total distribution costs and per bike cost for regular and premium bikes using the current costing system of the company.
b) Use ABC system to derive the above costs.
c) How can the ABC system help changing product decisions of the company?

Solution:

a) Total distribution cost = $4,260,000

Distribution cost per bike = $4,260,000 / (240,000 + 160,000) = $10.65 per bike

Below are the total distribution costs for each category of bikes:

	Regular		Premium	
	Total	Per Unit	Total	Per Unit
Distribution costs				
$10.65 * 240,000				
$10.65 * 160,000	$2,556,000.00	$10.65	$1,704,000.00	$10.65

b) If ABC system is used, the distribution costs would be allocated to multiple indirect-cost pools – marketing, order handling and delivery. Then using three different cost-allocation bases the costs would be allocated to the two products. Below is the calculation:

	Regular		Premium	
	Total	Per Unit	Total	Per Unit
Marketing costs	$160,000.00	$0.67	$480,000.00	$3.00
$16,000 * 10				
$16,000 * 30				
Order handling costs	$60,000.00	$0.25	$360,000.00	$2.25
$600 * 10 * 10				
$600 * 20 * 30				
Delivery costs				
$8 * 240,000	$1,920,000.00	$8.00	$1,280,000.00	$8.00
$8 * 160,000				
Total Indirect costs	$2,140,000.00	$8.92	$2,120,000.00	$13.25

c) Below is a comparison of the allocation of distribution costs to the two products based on the two different costing systems:

	Current system	ABC system
Regular	$10.65	$8.92
Premium	$10.65	$13.25

Using the costing information from the ABC system, the company knows that the Indirect costs of the Regular bikes are lower than those of the Premium bikes. It can use this information to take decisions, like select product-mix for higher profitability and try to reduce costs at the appropriate places (for example, try to reduce the marketing and order handling costs of Premium bikes as these seem much higher than the Regular bikes).

4.2 ZZZ Inc. is a retailer selling gents shirts, ladies shirts and unisex t-shirts. Following are the activities it identifies as indirect-cost pools:

Ordering	$1,000 per purchase order
Delivery	$800 per delivery
Shelf-stocking	$200 per hour
Billing	$2 per item sold

Following are the various other revenue, cost and activity usage of each product line:

	Gents Shirts	Ladies Shirts	Unisex T-Shirts
Revenue	$550,000	$650,000	$500,000
Cost of goods sold	$350,000	$450,000	$350,000
Support costs (non-ABC)	$105,000	$135,000	$105,000
Activity details:			
Purchase orders	30	25	15
Deliveries	100	30	25
Shelf-stocking hours	200	175	50
Items sold	15,000	20,000	10,000

a) **Using the support costs, without an ABC costing system (non-ABC support costs) find out the operating income of each product line.**

b) **Using ABC system compute operating income of each product line.**

c) **How can the company use this information to make an improvement?**

Solution:

a) Below is the income statement per product using non-ABC cost system:

	Gents Shirts	Ladies Shirts	Unisex T-Shirts
Revenue	$550,000	$650,000	$500,000
Cost of goods sold	$350,000	$450,000	$350,000
Gross profit	$200,000	$200,000	$150,000
Support costs	$105,000	$135,000	$105,000
Operating Income	$95,000	$65,000	$45,000
Operating margin	17.27%	10.00%	9.00%

b) When ABC system is used, the support costs would be allocated using the four indirect-cost allocation bases identified. They will be allocated to individual products using the cost-allocation bases as below:

	Gents Shirts	Ladies Shirts	Unisex T-Shirts
Revenue	$550,000	$650,000	$500,000
Cost of goods sold	$350,000	$450,000	$350,000
Gross profit	$200,000	$200,000	$150,000
Ordering costs			
$1,000 * 30	$30,000		
$1,000 * 25		$25,000	
$1,000 * 15			$15,000
Delivery costs			
$800 * 100	$80,000		
$800 * 30		$24,000	
$800 * 25			$20,000
Shelf-stocking costs			
$200 * 200	$40,000		
$200 * 175		$35,000	
$200 * 50			$10,000
Billing cost			
$2 * 15,000	$30,000		
$2 * 20,000		$40,000	
$2 * 10,000			$20,000
Total indirect costs	$180,000	$124,000	$65,000
Operating Income	$20,000	$76,000	$85,000
Operating margin	3.64%	11.69%	17.00%

c) By looking at the ABC costing the company would find that Unisex T-Shirts are the most profitable product line and Gents Shirts are the least. It can then try to increase its sales of Unisex T-Shirts and try to reduce some costs incurred on Gents Shirts. Delivery costs of Gents Shirts seem to be especially high due to more deliveries. It can try to reduce the number of deliveries to cut that cost.

Practice Exercises

4.1 AAA Inc. has two categories of overheads – maintenance and inspection. Costs expected for these categories for the coming year are as follows:

Maintenance: $360,000

Inspection: $750,000

The plant currently applies overheads using direct labor hours and the expected capacity is 100,000 direct labor hours. The following data has been assembled for use in developing a bid for a proposed job. Bid prices are calculated as full manufacturing cost plus a 20% mark-up.

Direct materials	$2,100
Direct labor	$5,625
Machine hours	450
Number of inspections	4
Direct labor hours	550

Total expected machine hours for all jobs during the year are 60,000 and the total expected number of inspections is 4,000.

a) Compute the total cost of the potential job using direct labor hours to assign overhead. Determine the bid price for the potential job.

b) Compute the total cost of the job using activity-based costing and the appropriate activity drivers. Determine the bid price if activity-based costing is used.

4.2 XYZ Inc. produces two types of watches – low-end and high-end. Data related to the two products is as below:

	Low-end	High-end
Production	50,000	100,000
Direct materials costs	$150,000	$300,000
Direct labor costs	$75,000	$175,000
Direct manufacturing labor hours	3,000	4,500
Machine hours	10,000	18,000
Number of lots produced	100	100
Inspection effort (hours)	500	750

The combined manufacturing overhead costs are as follows:

Machining costs	$400,000
Setup costs (depend on lots produced)	$100,000
Inspection costs	$100,000

a) Compute manufacturing overhead costs per unit for each product.

b) Compute manufacturing cost per unit for each product.

c) If the company uses a mark-up of 30%, compute the selling price for each product.

d) Identify the main cost drivers for each product. How can the company reduce costs of manufacturing each product?

4.3 ZZZ Inc. distributes medicines to pharmacists and doctors. Following are the activities:

Activity	Rate
Taking order	$400 per order
Billing	$30 per item in order
Delivering order	$500 per delivery
Packaging	$10 per package
Stocking	$150 per hour

The customer profitability of the two customers is to be computed using the data below:

	Pharmacist	Doctor
Total orders	10	10
Average items per order	15	20
Total deliveries	5	10
Average packages per delivery	20	15
Average stocking time per delivery	1 hour	1.5 hours

a) Compute the Operating Income per customer.

b) Comment on the findings and suggest steps to improve customer profitability.

This page is intentionally left blank.

CHAPTER 5:

Support Department Cost Allocation

Every company has two types of departments – operating departments and support departments. Operating departments are those that directly add value to the product or service provided by the company. Support departments provide services that assist other departments internal to the company.

Need for Cost Allocation

All direct costs are traced to the products or services. However, without allocating the support department costs or overheads, the costs could be misleading. Below sections show the decisions that could go wrong if support department costs are not correctly allocated.

Pricing Decisions

Companies use costs as the floor for pricing decisions. Any price above the cost brings profits to the company. If support department costs (indirect costs) are not allocated, it could give lower cost for the company's products or services, thereby leading to incorrect pricing decisions.

Product / Department Profitability

Companies are always on the lookout to promote their more profitable products and services and improve upon or discontinue low profitable or loss making products and services. Similarly, companies take decisions to grow or divest operating departments based on the profitability of those departments. Unless the indirect costs are properly allocated, it will not be possible to get a complete picture of product, service or department profitability.

Cost Allocation Basis

Support department costs are generally allocated using one of the below two criteria:

a) Cause and effect – when indirect costs are easy to allocate to operating departments based on their usage, cause and effect criteria is used. For example, allocation of computer support department costs to operating departments can be based on the computer time used by them.

b) Benefits received – indirect costs are allocated to operating departments based on the benefits they are expected to receive. For example, the costs of a marketing campaign could be allocated based on how much each operating department is expected to benefit from the promotion.

Allocating Costs of One Support Department

When there is just one support department in a company, its costs can be allocated to operating departments using two methods – Single-Rate method and Dual-Rate method. The difference between the two methods is the way they treat fixed and variable costs.

Single-Rate & Dual-Rate Methods

When Single-Rate method is used to allocate support department costs, the costs are not converted into fixed and variable. Instead a single total cost is used and directly allocated to the operating departments. The basis for allocating costs can be on budgeted (or actual) usage or total capacity. Below sections give an example of each of the basis.

For Dual-Rate method the support department costs are classified into fixed and variable and allocated separately. The basis for allocation is similar to Single-Rate method.

Consider an example of a company that has one support department – information technology department, and two operating departments – software services and hardware products. The support department provides computer services to the operating departments and the capacity is on the basis of computer hours available. Below are the support department costs, budgeted hours of usage and actual hours of usage by the operating departments:

Capacity of information technology department
     20,000 hours
Fixed costs of information technology department
     $50,000,000
Budgeted hours of usage of information technology department:
     Software services operating department
     9,000 hours
     Hardware products operating department
     <u>6,000 hours</u>

Total

15,000 hours

Budgeted variable costs per hour

$100

Actual hours of usage of information technology department:

Software services operating department

11,000 hours

Hardware products operating department

4,000 hours

Total

15,000 hours

Allocation based on Budgeted (or Actual) Usage

Using Single-Rate method, the fixed and variable costs are added together to find the total cost of the support department. Then the total cost per hour is calculated based on budgeted hours. Finally, the total cost to be allocated to each operating department is calculated using the actual hours used. Shown below is the complete cost allocation using Single-Rate method:

Budgeted Total cost ($50,000,000 + $100 * 15,000 hours) = $51,500,000

Budgeted rate per hour ($51,500,000 / 15,000 hours) = $3,433.33

Allocation to Software services department ($3,433.33 * 11,000 hours) = $37,766,666

Allocation to Hardware products department ($3,433.33 * 4,000 hours) = $13,733,333

Using the Dual-Rate method, fixed cost per hour is computed using budgeted hours. The fixed and variable costs per hour are then used separately with the actual hours used to compute the total fixed and variable costs to be allocated to the operating departments separately. Budgeted hours are used with fixed costs, whereas, actual hours are used with variable costs. Shown below is the complete cost allocation using Dual-Rate method:

Fixed cost per hour ($50,000,000 / 15,000 hours) = $3,333.33
Fixed costs allocated to Software services department
($3,333.33 * 9,000 hours) = $30,000,000
Variable costs allocated to Software services department ($100 * 11,000) = $1,100,000
Total costs allocated to Software services department =
$31,100,000
Fixed costs allocated to Hardware products department
($3,333.33 * 6,000 hours) = $20,000,000
Variable costs allocated to Hardware products department
($100 * 4,000) = $400,000
Total costs allocated to Hardware products department =
$20,400,000

As seen above, although the support department cost allocated to the two operating departments is quite different between the two methods, the total cost allocated is the same. This will always be the case as the support department cost incurred is the same, irrespective of the method used.

Allocation based on Total Capacity

This method uses the total capacity of the support department to allocate the fixed costs. This helps in unearthing how much capacity is unutilized within the support department. It also leaves some residual cost of the support department as the allocation of costs to operating departments is not complete. This residual cost can be used by managers of that department to take decision on reducing capacity to save costs.

Once again the Single-Rate method or the Dual-Rate method is used as below:

Fixed cost per hour ($50,000,000 / 20,000 hours) = $2,500

Variable cost per hour = $100

Using Single-Rate method

Budgeted rate per hour ($2,500 + $100) = $2,600
Allocation to Software services department ($2,600 * 11,000 hours) = $28,600,000
Allocation to Hardware products department ($2,600 * 4,000 hours) = $10,400,000
Unallocated ($2,600 * 5,000 hours) = $13,000,000

Using Dual-Rate method

Fixed costs allocated to Software services department ($2,500 * 9,000 hours) = $22,500,000
Variable costs allocated to Software services department ($100 * 11,000) = $1,100,000

Total costs allocated to Software services department =
$23,600,000

Fixed costs allocated to Hardware products department ($2,500
* 6,000 hours) = $15,000,000

Variable costs allocated to Hardware products department
($100 * 4,000) = $400,000

Total costs allocated to Hardware products department =
$15,400,000

Unallocated ($2,600 * 5,000 hours) = $13,000,000

As seen above, there will be costs that would remain
unallocated. This data helps managers find departments that
have excess capacity that is not used. They may use this data to
take appropriate capacity reduction decisions to save costs.

Allocating Costs of Multiple Support Departments

When there are multiple support departments, the cost
allocation could be more complex as support departments may
provide service to other support departments. There are three
methods of allocation of support department costs when
multiple support departments are present.

Direct Method

In this method costs of support departments are directly
allocated to the operating departments. Even though the

support departments provide services to each other, there is no cost allocation between them. Hence, this method is very simple for cost allocation. Below is an example of a company with two support departments and two operating departments.

| | Support Departments | | Operating Departments | | |
	Maintenance	Computer Systems	Production	Packaging	Total
Budgeted overhead costs	$50,000	$100,000	$30,000	$40,000	$220,000
Support work done:					
By Maintenance					
Budgeted labor-hours	-	2,800	7,000	4,200	14,000
Percentage	-	20%	50%	30%	100%
By Computer Systems					
Budgeted computer hours	500	-	2,000	2,500	5,000
Percentage	10%	-	40%	50%	100%

In the above data we see that both support departments provide services to each other as well. In Direct Method, we start allocation of support department costs to operating departments independent of this fact. Let's start with the Maintenance department. Its services are divided in the following ratio between the two operating departments based on budgeted labor-hours:

Allocation to Production department: 50% / (50% + 30%) = 5/8
Allocation to Packaging department: 30% / (50% + 30%) = 3/8

Similarly, computer systems services are divided as below based on budgeted computer hours:

Allocation to Production department: 40% / (40% + 50%) = 4/9
Allocation to Packaging department: 50% / (40% + 50%) = 5/9

Below are the calculations:

| | Support Departments | | Operating Departments | |
| | | Computer | | |
	Maintenance	Systems	Production	Packaging
Budgeted overhead costs	$50,000	$100,000	$30,000	$40,000
Allocation of Maintenance costs (5/8, 3/8)	($50,000) -		$31,250	$18,750
Allocation of Computer Systems costs (4/9, 5/9)	-	($100,000)	$44,444	$55,556
Total overhead of operating departments	$0	$0	$105,694	$114,306

Below is a diagrammatic representation of the above cost allocation:

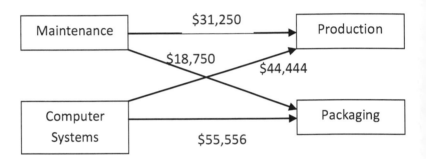

Step-Down Method

Using this method support department costs are allocated to operating departments as well as other support departments. Sequence of allocation is then important. We start with the support department that provides more services to other support departments. In the above example, Maintenance provides 20% services to Computer Systems, whereas, Computer Systems provides only 10% services to Maintenance. Hence, we start with Maintenance first. Below are the allocation ratios for Maintenance:

Allocation to Computer Systems department: 20% / (20% + 50% + 30%) = 2/10

Allocation to Production department: 50% / (20% + 50% + 30%) = 5/10

Allocation to Packaging department: 30% / (20% + 50% + 30%) = 3/10

Allocation of the Computer Systems department happens using the same ratio as above as there is no further allocation from Computer Systems to Maintenance. Below are the calculations:

| | Support Departments | | Operating Departments | |
| | | Computer | | |
	Maintenance	Systems	Production	Packaging
Budgeted overhead costs	$50,000	$100,000	$30,000	$40,000
Allocation of Maintenance costs (2/10, 5/10, 3/10)	($50,000)	$10,000	$25,000	$15,000
		$110,000		
Allocation of Computer Systems costs (4/9, 5/9)	-	($110,000)	$48,889	$61,111
Total overhead of operating departments	$0	$0	$103,889	$116,111

Below is a diagrammatic representation of the above cost allocation:

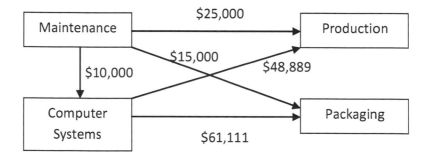

Reciprocal Method

In this method the support departments allocate costs to other support departments and operating departments over and over again until all costs have been allocated. So in the above case, Maintenance would allocate to Computer Systems, Production and Packaging. Then Computer Systems would allocate to Maintenance, Production and Packaging and so on, until all support department costs have been completely allocated. In order to simplify this long procedure, mathematical equations are used based on allocation between the support departments. For the above example, the following two equations would be used:

$M = \$50,000 + 0.1CS$
$CS = \$100,000 + 0.2M$

Where, M stands for Maintenance department costs & CS stands for costs of Computer Systems department.
Solving the two equations gives
$M = \$50,000 + 0.1 * (\$100,000 + 0.2M) = \$50,000 + \$10,000 + 0.02M$
$= \$60,000 + 0.02M$
Therefore, $M = \$60,000 / 0.98 = \$61,224.5$
And $CS = \$100,000 + 0.2 * \$61,224.5 = \$112,244.9$

These values are then used to allocate to the operating departments as below:

| | Support Departments | | Operating Departments | |
	Maintenance	Computer Systems	Production	Packaging
Budgeted overhead costs	$50,000	$100,000	$30,000	$40,000
Allocation of Maintenance costs (2/10, 5/10, 3/10)	($61,225)	$12,245	$30,612	$18,367
Allocation of Computer Systems costs (1/10, 4/10, 5/10)	$11,224	($112,245)	$44,898	$56,122
Total overhead of operating departments	($0)	$0	$105,510	$114,490

The only difference between this method and the Step-Down method is that the allocation of support department costs is not done using the overhead of that department. Instead, an amount is computed using the equations first based on the inter-department allocation and that amount is used for allocating the costs of one support department at a time.

Below is a diagrammatic representation of the above cost allocation:

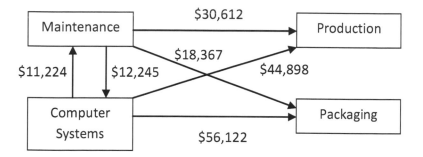

Solved Examples

5.1 AAA Inc. has four operating departments (A, B, C & D) and one support department, P. The manufacturing departments take power from the support department based on the below capacity and expected usage:

Operating Department	Required Capacity of P (in KWh)	Expected Usage of P (in KWh)
A	10,000	8,000
B	20,000	9,000
C	12,000	7,000
D	8,000	6,000
Total	50,000	30,000

The total cost of department P is $1,500,000, out of which $600,000 is variable and 900,000 is fixed.

a) Compute the allocation of support department costs to the operating departments using Single-Rate method based on required capacity.

b) Use the Dual-Rate method to allocate the support department cost. Allocate fixed cost based on required capacity and variable cost based on expected usage.

Solution:

a) Single-Rate method has only one cost pool as below:

Total cost = $1,500,000

Total required capacity = 50,000 KWh

Cost per KWh = $1,500,000 / 50,000 = $30 per KWh

Below are the cost allocations:

	A	B	C	D
Required Capacity	10,000	20,000	12,000	8,000
Cost allocated (@$30 / KWh)	$ 300,000.00	$ 600,000.00	$ 360,000.00	$ 240,000.00

b) Dual-Rate method differentiates between fixed and variable costs. We are required to use required capacity for allocating fixed costs and expected usage for allocating variable costs. Below are the cost pools:

Fixed cost = $900,000

Total required capacity = 50,000 KWh

Fixed cost per KWh = $900,000 / $50,000 = $18 per KWh

Variable cost = $600,000

Total expected usage = 30,000 KWh

Variable cost per KWh = $600,000 / 30,000 = $20 per KWh

Below are the cost allocations:

	A	B	C	D
Required Capacity	10,000	20,000	12,000	8,000
Fixed Cost allocated (@$18 / KWh)	$ 180,000.00	$ 360,000.00	$ 216,000.00	$ 144,000.00
Expected Usage	8,000	9,000	7,000	6,000
Variable Cost allocated (@20 / KWh)	$ 160,000.00	$ 180,000.00	$ 140,000.00	$ 120,000.00
Total Cost allocated	$ 340,000.00	$ 540,000.00	$ 356,000.00	$ 264,000.00

5.2 XYZ Inc. has two operating departments and two support departments. Below is the data related to costs and other relevant details of these departments:

Department	Revenue	Cost	No. of employees	Pages printed
Wholesale Sales	$1,334,200	$998,270	42	1,920
Retail Sales	$667,100	$489,860	28	1,600
HR	-	$72,700	14	320
Printing	-	$234,400	21	1,120

Use the number of employees to allocate cost of HR department and pages printed to allocate cost of Printing department.

a) Allocate support department cost using Direct method.

b) Use Reciprocal method to do the cost allocation.

Solution:

a) In Direct method, the costs of the two support departments are allocated to the operating departments without any allocation to each other.

Let's start with the HR department. Its services are divided in the following ratio between the two operating departments based on budgeted labor-hours:

Allocation to Wholesale Sales department: 42 / (42 + 28) = 0.6

Allocation to Retail Sales department: 28 / (42 + 28) = 0.4

Similarly, Printing department costs are divided as below based on pages printed:

Allocation to Wholesale Sales department: 1,920 / (1,920 + 1,600) = 0.545

Allocation to Retail Sales department: 1,600 / (1,920 + 1,600) = 0.455

Below are the calculations:

	Support Departments		Operating Departments	
			Wholesale	Retail
	HR	Printing	Sales	Sales
Budgeted overhead costs	$72,700	$234,400	$998,270	$489,860
Allocation of HR costs (0.6, 0.4))	($72,700)	-	$43,620	$29,080
Allocation of Printing costs (0.545, 0.455)	-	($234,400)	$127,748	$106,652
Total overhead of operating departments	$0	$0	$1,169,638	$625,592

b) To use the Reciprocal method, we need to make two equations representing the allocation of support department costs on each other as below:

HR = $72,700 + (320 / (1,920 + 1,600 + 320)) * P = $72,700 + 0.08333P

P = $234,400 + (21 / (42 + 28 + 21)) * HR = $234,400 + 0.23077HR

Solving the above equations:

HR = $72,700 + 0.08333 * ($234,400 + 0.23077HR) = $72,700 + $19,532.55 + 0.01923HR

Hence, HR = $92,232.55 / 0.98077 = $94,041

And P = $234,400 + 0.23077 * $94,041 = $256,102

Shown below are the cost allocations using this method:

	Support Departments		Operating Departments	
			Wholesale	Retail
	HR	Printing	Sales	Sales
Budgeted overhead costs	$72,700	$234,400	$998,270	$489,860
Allocation of HR costs (21/91, 42/91, 28/91)	($94,041)	$21,702	$43,404	$28,936
Allocation of Printing costs (320/3,840, 1,920 / 3,840, 1,600 / 3,840)	$21,342	($256,102)	$128,051	$106,709
Total overhead of operating departments	$1	($0)	$1,169,725	$625,505

There is some residual value left in the support departments due to rounding off error.

Practice Exercises

5.1 Describe the differences between support and operating departments. Give two examples of each.

5.2 ZZZ Inc. prices its products at full cost plus 30%. The company operates two support departments and two operating departments. Budgeted costs and normal activity levels are as follows:

	Support Departments		Operating Departments	
	W	X	Y	Z
Overhead costs	$40,000	$100,000	$180,000	$240,000
Square feet	1,000	1,200	2,000	6,000
No of employees	20	30	60	40
Labor hours	-	-	10,000	6,400
Machine hours	-	-	6,000	10,800

Support department W's costs are allocated based on square feet and support department X's costs are allocated based on number of employees.

a) Use Direct method of cost allocation to find the overheads allocated to each operating department.

b) Department Y uses labor hours to assign overhead costs to products while department Z uses machine hours. One of the products the company produces requires 4 labor hours per unit in department Y and no time in department Z. Direct materials for the product cost $180 per unit and direct labor is $80 per unit. Compute the selling price of the company's product based on the above pricing policy.

CHAPTER 6:

Cost Control

Every company creates a budget that serves as a baseline for their business. They also compare the actual performance with the budgeted planned performance and calculate variances. A variance is any deviation from the budget.

Companies create mainly three kinds of budgets. The first one is for revenue; second is for the Direct costs and third is for the Indirect costs. Variances against each of these are calculated differently. Sections below show which variances are calculated and how to interpret them.

Direct Variances

There are two kinds of direct variances – revenue and cost. Both are described in the sections below.

Revenue Variance

All companies create a budget of how much of which product or service they would sell in the year and at what price. This is shown as below:

Budgeted Revenue = Price * Quantity

If there is a deviation in the revenue, it leads to a Revenue Variance as below:

Total Revenue Variance = Actual Revenue – Budgeted Revenue

This variance could occur due to less or more quantity sold and/or less or more price of each unit. Hence, the above total revenue variance can actually be broken into two parts as below:

Total Revenue Variance = Revenue Quantity Variance + Revenue Price Variance

The revenue quantity variance is due to difference between the budgeted and actual quantities. The revenue price variance is due to difference between the budgeted and actual prices. The two variances are as given below:

Revenue Quantity Variance = (AQ – SQ) * SP

Revenue Price Variance = (AP – SP) * AQ

Where,

AQ is Actual quantity

SQ is Standard (or budgeted) quantity

AP is Actual price

SP is Standard (or budgeted) price

Hence, Total Revenue Variance = (AQ – SQ) * SP + (AP – SP) * AQ

= AQ*SP – SQ*SP + AP*AQ – SP*AQ = AP*AQ - SQ*SP = Actual revenue – Budgeted revenue

In the above equation, SQ*SP stands for Standard (or budgeted) revenue and AP*AQ stands for Actual revenue. It may also be noted that while calculating quantity variance we use the standard price and with price variance we use actual quantity. This is the most frequently used way of computing variances but it can also be done the other way.

Let's take an example. Consider a company selling only one product. It has created a revenue budget as below:

	Standard (or budgeted)	Actual
Quantity	1,000 (SQ)	950 (AQ)
Price	$40 (SP)	$50 (AP)

Total Revenue Variance = (950 * $50) – (1,000 * $40) = $47,500 – $40,000 = $7,500 (F)

As seen above, the total revenue variance is favourable by $7,500. This is because the company has managed to earn revenue that is more than it budgeted for. However, the complete story is not yet known unless the individual variances are also calculated. Below are those calculations.

Revenue Quantity Variance = (950 – 1,000) * $40 = -$2,000 (U)

Revenue Price Variance = ($50 - $40) * 950 = $9,500 (F)

The individual variances reveal that the company sold less quantity (an unfavourable variance) at a higher price (a favourable variance). This may mean that the sales team decided to increase the selling price of the product at the expense of losing some sales. But it had overall given a favourable outcome to the company's revenues.

Direct Cost Variance

Every product or service has two types of costs – direct and indirect. The direct costs are generally direct labor and direct material costs. Any variance in the budgeted quantity of materials used, labor used or their rates can give a direct cost variance. These variances are very similar to revenue variance seen earlier. The Total Direct Cost Variance is as given below:

Total Direct Cost Variance = Actual Direct Costs – Standard (or budgeted) Direct Costs

This variance can be caused due to the below factors:

a) Quantity of direct materials used (using less or more quantity of raw materials)
b) Price of direct materials used (buying raw materials at a lower or higher price)
c) Quantity of direct labor used (using less or more quantity of labor)
d) Price of direct labor used (hiring labor at a lower or higher price)

Accordingly, the total direct cost variance can be split into four components. Let's first see each of these components individually below.

When a company uses a raw material lesser than it budgeted for, it will save money – it will have favourable Material Usage Variance given below.

Material Usage Variance = (SQ – AQ) * SP

Where, SQ, AQ & SP are all standard and actual values for direct materials used

Similarly, when the company uses more labor than budgeted for, it will spend more money – it will have unfavourable Labor Efficiency Variance given below.

Labor Efficiency Variance = (SQ – AQ) * SP (Note: this is similar to material usage variance)

Where, SQ, AQ & SP are all standard and actual values for direct labor used

In the same way there can be two price variances due to difference between budgeted and actual price of the raw materials or labor as below.

Purchase Price Variance = (SP – AP) * AQ

Where, SP, AP & AQ are all standard and actual values for direct materials used

Labor Rate Variance = (SP – AP) * AQ (Note: this is similar to purchase price variance)

Where, SP, AP & AQ are all standard and actual values for direct labor used

The total variance is then given as:

Total Direct Cost Variance = Material Usage Variance + Labor Efficiency Variance + Purchase Price Variance + Labor Rate Variance

Let's take an example to illustrate the Direct cost variances. Assume a company that produces woollen jackets. The only raw material used is wool. From the past data the company creates a direct cost budget for the next year as below (this is to make one jacket):

	Quantity	Price	Standard (or budgeted)
Wool	5 yarns (SQ - materials)	$2 (SP - materials)	$10
Labor	3 hours (SQ - labor)	$10 (SP - labor)	$30
Total			$40

At the end of the year the company gathers the actual values as below:

	Quantity	Price	Actual
Wool	4.5 yarns (AQ – materials)	$2.25 (AP – materials)	$10.125
Labor	2 hours (AQ – labor)	$12 (AP – labor)	$24
Total			$34.125

If the company simply calculates the total direct cost variance then it gets:

Total Direct Cost Variance = $40 - $34.125 = $5.875 (F)

Although the company has a favourable variance, it is not the end of the story as the company still does not know which departments performed well. In order to know that it needs to compute the individual direct material and direct labor variances as below.

Material Usage Variance = (5 – 4.5) * $2 = $1 (F)

Labor Efficiency Variance = (3 – 2) * $10 = $10 (F)

Purchase Price Variance = ($2 - $2.25) * 4.5 = -$1.125 (U)

Labor Rate Variance = ($10 - $12) * 2 = -$4 (U)

Now it is clearer to understand which department of the company has performed well and which has not and how much each contributed to the favourable total variance. From the above example, it seems like the company did well in reducing the use of raw materials which could be due to reduction in waste. The company also took lesser time, showing increase in employee productivity. However, the company spent more money in buying raw materials and also in hiring labor – possibly due to temporary labor or multiple shifts that work out costlier. The individual variance information helps the company analyze areas of concern so as to take corrective action.

Indirect Variances

Most companies have Indirect costs. They are all the overhead costs like, rent, depreciation, power etc. Variances of these costs are more difficult to compute as they cannot be easily traced to the product or service. There are two ways to compute variances of such costs.

Fixed Budgeting

In this approach, all the overhead (or indirect) costs are budgeted using the expected sales volume. No matter how much the actual sales are, the variances are calculated using this fixed budget only.

For example, consider the below budgeted overhead costs:

Item	Budgeted Cost	Type of Cost
Rent	$10,000	Fixed
Depreciation	$20,000	Fixed
Power	$5,000	Semi-variable
Office supplies	$500	Semi-variable
Plant supervision	$1,000	Step cost
Total	$36,500	

Some of the above costs are purely fixed, whereas, others are semi-variable. Rent and depreciation are fixed overheads that do not vary with the production volume. However, power, office supplies and plant supervision may vary with production volume – they are either semi-variable or a step cost. A step cost is the one that is fixed over a certain relevant range, beyond which it changes in a lump. Plant supervision is one such cost. Until, say, 120% of the expected production, the plant may do with a single supervisor. But if the production goes beyond that, another supervisor needs to be hired until the production goes beyond 200%.

In the above example, the overheads are budgeted for a normal production volume of 100,000 units. Now, if the number of units produced in the year is 150,000, then the semi-variable costs – power and office supplies will go up. This may make the company believe that they have spent more on power than budgeted and that the variance is unfavourable. But in reality it is only because of more production. Similar cases can happen with plant supervision, which is a step-cost. Hence, this method would lead to incorrect conclusions. This happens because this method treats all overheads as fixed costs.

Flexible Budgeting

This method gives due credit to overhead costs that are not fixed. Instead of having a single fixed budget for overheads, the company prepares several budgets based on varying levels of production as below:

Capacity Utilization ->	60%	70%	80%	100%
Units Produced ->	60,000	70,000	80,000	100,000
Rent	$10,000	$10,000	$10,000	$10,000
Depreciation	$20,000	$20,000	$20,000	$20,000
Power	$4,000	$4,200	$4,500	$5,000
Office supplies	$425	$450	$475	$500
Plant supervision	$500	$1,000	$1,000	$1,500
Total	$34,925	$35,650	$35,975	$37,000

Now, depending upon the capacity utilization for the year, the appropriate flexible budget is used to compute the variances. This gives a much more realistic picture of variances. The Total at each level of production is called the Allowed Overhead. The overhead the company actually incurs at budgeted capacity (assume 100% in this case) is called the Actual Overhead. Finally, the overhead cost included or absorbed in the products is called Absorbed Overhead. Below are examples from above data:

At 60% capacity utilization

Allowed Overhead = $34,925

Actual Overhead = $37,000

Absorbed Overhead - Is computed based on how much has been included in each product that is sold. For example if 1,000 units of a product are sold and each unit includes an Indirect cost of $35, then absorbed overhead is $35,000.

At 70% capacity utilization

Allowed Overhead = $35,650

Actual Overhead = $37,000

At 80% capacity utilization

Allowed Overhead = $35,975

Actual Overhead = $37,000

At 100% capacity utilization

Allowed Overhead = $37,000

Actual Overhead = $37,000

Total Variance = Actual Overhead − Absorbed Overhead

It has two components as below:

Volume Variance = Allowed Overhead − Absorbed Overhead

Spending Variance = Actual Overhead − Allowed Overhead

Hence, Total Variance = Volume Variance + Spending Variance

Solved Examples

6.1 AAA Inc. has budgeted the direct materials, direct manufacturing labor and direct distribution cost per consignment as $100, $50 and $70 respectively. The actual performance is as below:

	Actual Costs
Direct Materials	$900,000
Direct manufacturing labor	$450,000
Direct distribution	$500,000

The above actual costs are with an actual output of 8,000 units of the product as against the budgeted output of 10,000 units.

a) Compute the Direct variances for the company.
b) Comment on the variances.

Solution:

a) The actual costs are incurred for 8,000 units. We can compute per unit cost of each cost item (direct materials, direct manufacturing labor, direct distribution) as below:

	Total Costs	Per Unit Cost
Direct Materials	$900,000.00	$112.50
Direct manufacturing labor	$450,000.00	$56.25
Direct distribution	$500,000.00	$62.50

The above per unit costs are compared with the budgeted costs below along with the individual variances:

	Actual	Budgeted	Variance	Type
Direct Materials	$112.50	$100.00	($12.50)	Unfavourable
Direct manufacturing labor	$56.25	$50.00	($6.25)	Unfavourable
Direct distribution	$62.50	$70.00	$7.50	Favourable
Total	$231.25	$220.00	($11.25)	Unfavourable

b) There are unfavourable variances on direct materials and direct manufacturing labor. This means that the company has spent more than budgeted in these two direct cost items. The direct distribution variance is favourable, pointing towards spend that is lower than the budgeted value.

6.2 XYZ Inc. buys internet access time from other companies in bulk to sell to its retail customers. It budgets to buy 80,000 minutes at $0.05 per minute. However, the actual purchases through the year are 100,000 minutes at $0.065 per minute due to increased demand. The company also budgets to pay $15 per hour to workers for installation of services. Installation effort is budgeted to be 1 hour for 500 minutes of internet access time. The actual rate it pays to workers is $14.50 and it pays for a total of 180 hours.

a) Compute direct material variances.

b) Compute direct labor variances.

c) Compute total direct cost variance.

Solution:

a) Direct material budgets and actual are directly given and the variances are calculated as below:

Material usage variance = (SQ – AQ) * SP = (80,000 – 100,000) * $0.05 = -$1,000 (U)
Purchase Price variance = (SP – AP) * AQ = ($0.05 - $0.065) * 100,000 = -$1,500 (U)

b) Direct labor variances are calculated as below:

Labor efficiency variance = (SQ – AQ) * SP
SQ = 1 hour * (80,000 / 500 minutes) = 160 hours
AQ = 180 hours
Therefore, Labor efficiency variance = (160 – 180) * $15 = -$300 (U)
Labor rate variance = (SP – AP) * AQ = ($15 - $14.50) * 180 = $90 (F)

c) Total direct cost variance = (-$1,000) + (-$1,500) + (-$300) + $90 = -$2,710

6.3 ZZZ Inc. manufactures with a monthly normal production of 10,000 units. Standard factory overhead rate are based on a normal monthly volume of one standard hour per unit. Standard factory rates per direct labor hour are:

Fixed	$6.00
Variable	$10.00

Units actually produced in the current month are 9,000. Actual factory overhead costs incurred (includes $70,000 fixed) are $156,000. Actual direct labor hours are 9,000.

a) What is the variable overhead spending variance for the company?

Solution:

a) Variable overhead spending variance = Actual variable overhead – Allowed variable overhead

Actual variable overhead = $156,000 - $70,000 = $86,000
Allowed variable overhead = 9,000 * $10 = 90,000

Therefore,

Variable overhead spending variance = $86,000 - $90,000 = -$4,000 (F)

The above variance is favourable since the actual is lower than allowed. This means that the company has spent less than it was allowed to spend on the variable overheads at 9,000 units of production.

Practice Exercises

6.1 AAA Inc. manufactures 100-pound bags of fertilizers that have the following unit standard costs for direct materials and direct labor:

Direct materials (100 lbs @ $1.00 per lb)	$100.00
Direct labor (0.5 hours @ $24 per hour)	$12.00
Total standard direct cost per 100 lb bag	$112.00

The following activities were recorded for the month:
1,000 bags were manufactured
95,000 lbs. Of materials costing $76,000 were purchased
102,500 lbs. Of materials were used
$12,000 was paid for 475 hours of direct labor

There was no beginning or ending work-in-process inventories.

a) Compute direct material variances.
b) Compute direct labor variances.
c) Give possible reasons for the occurrence of each of the preceding variances.

6.2 XYZ Inc. makes chocolates. For the month it budgeted to purchase and use 15,000 lb of cocoa at $17.80. Actual purchase and usage was 16,000 lb at $16.40. It had

budgeted for 3,750 lb of chocolates. Actual output was
3,800 lb of chocolates.

a) Compute direct material variances.
b) Comment on the performance of the company.

6.3 ZZZ Inc. has a capacity of 5,000 units. Standard factory
overhead rate is based on a normal monthly volume of 0.5
standard hour per unit. Standard factory variable rate per
hour is $50. Units actually produced in the current month
are 4,500. Actual factory variable overhead costs incurred
are $100,000. Actual direct labor hours are 2,250.

a) What is the variable overhead spending variance for
the company?

This page is intentionally left blank.

Glossary

Absorbed overhead – the amount of overhead costs that have been absorbed by the products and services sold by a company

Actual overhead – the amount of overhead costs that have actually been incurred by a company

Allowed overhead – the amount of overhead costs that need to be included in the products and services of a company under flexible budgeting

Balance sheet - a financial statement that gives a snapshot of a company's resources (assets)/ obligations (liabilities)/ and owners' equity

Beginning inventory – the stock of raw materials, in-process materials and finished products held by a company at the start of the period (year / quarter)

Breakeven point (BEP) – the point at which a company's total revenues are equal to the total costs

Broad Averaging – a type of costing system that allocates Indirect costs to products/services/departments by averaging

Contribution income statement – a statement of a company's income that shows variable costs and fixed costs separately

Contribution margin – equals (Revenues – Variable costs)

Contribution margin percentage – equals (Contribution margin / Revenues)

Conversion costs – equals (Direct manufacturing labor costs + Manufacturing overhead costs)

Cost object – a product or a service to which costs need to be traced or allocated

Cost of goods manufactured – cost incurred in manufacturing products over the period (year / quarter)

Cost of goods sold – cost incurred in manufacturing products that were sold during the period (year / quarter), irrespective of when the products were manufactured

CVP analysis – an analysis that shows the relationship between costs, volume and profit

Direct costs – costs that can be cost effectively traced to a cost object

Direct cost variance – equals (Actual Direct Costs – Standard (or budgeted) Direct Costs)

Direct manufacturing labor costs – labor costs incurred in manufacturing a product that can be cost effectively traced to a cost object

Direct material costs – cost of raw materials incurred in manufacturing a product that can be cost effectively traced to a cost object

Direct method for support department cost allocation – a method of allocating Indirect costs of support departments to operating departments where no allocation is done from one support department to another

Direct variance – the difference between actual and standard (or budgeted) revenue or Direct costs

Dual-rate method for support department cost allocation – a method of allocating Indirect costs of support departments to operating departments by using separate pools for fixed and variable costs

Ending inventory - the stock of raw materials, in-process materials and finished products held by a company at the end of the period (year / quarter)

Fixed budgeting – a method of evaluating Indirect cost variance where the budgeted costs are held fixed, irrespective of the volume of production

Fixed costs – costs that do not change with the volume of production, generally over a relevant range

Flexible budgeting – a method of evaluating Indirect cost variance where the budgeted costs are computed on the basis of the volume of production

Gross profit – equals (Revenues – Cost of goods sold)

Income statement - reports the net income earned by a company over a period (year / quarter)

Indirect costs – costs that cannot be cost effectively traced to a cost object. These costs are allocated to cost objects.

Indirect manufacturing costs – costs of manufacturing that cannot be traced to a cost object

Indirect variance – the difference between actual and standard (or budgeted) Indirect costs

Inventoriable costs – costs that can be shown as an inventory in a company's balance sheet until a sale takes place

Inventory – stock of raw materials, in-process, and finished products held by a company until a sale takes place

Margin of safety – equals (Budgeted revenue – Breakeven revenue)

Net profit – the profit earned by a company after deducting all expenses from the revenues

Operating income – the income of a company before considering interest and income tax payments. Also called EBIT (Earnings Before Interest and Tax).

Operating leverage (Degree of operating leverage) – equals (Contribution margin / Operating income)

Opportunity cost – income forgone by choosing a particular alternative

Period costs – costs that cannot be inventorized and appear in a company's income statement in the period they were incurred

Prime costs – equals (Direct material costs + Direct manufacturing labor costs)

Reciprocal method of support department cost allocation - a method of allocating Indirect costs of support departments to operating departments where support department costs are allocated to each other over and over again before allocating them to operating departments

Revenue – money earned by a company on account of sales and other activities

Revenue variance - the difference between actual and standard (or budgeted) revenue

Semi-variable costs – costs that have a fixed cost component and a variable cost component

Single-rate method – a method of allocating Indirect costs of support departments to operating departments by using a single pool for both fixed and variable costs

Spending variance – equals (Actual overhead – Allowed overhead)

Step-down method - a method of allocating Indirect costs of support departments to operating departments where support department costs are allocated to each other once before allocating them to operating departments

Unit costs – cost of a single unit of the product or service

Variable costs – costs that change with the volume of production in direct proportion

Volume variance – equals (Allowed overhead – Absorbed overhead)

Made in the USA
Lexington, KY
14 October 2011